TURNING A TELEPHONE ANSWERING SERVICE INTO A CALL CENTER

PETER LYLE DEHAAN

Contents

ABSTRACT OF DISSERTATION

TURNING A TELEPHONE ANSWERING SERVICE INTO A CALL CENTER

by

Peter L. DeHaan

Kennedy-Western University

THE PROBLEM

The telephone answering service industry is maturing and undergoing rapid changes. In recent years, the traditional client has been vanishing, switching to alternative technologies, bypassing their answering service. Telephone answering services have reacted in various ways, such as mergers and acquisitions, pursuing niches, or expanding their businesses' scope.

The conventional wisdom is that there will always be a need for the human interaction which an answering service provides. It further assumes that answering services will serve fewer clients and generate

1

less revenue unless steps are taken to increase their reach or obtain non-traditional clients. Previous research has recommended becoming a call center to better tap and capitalize on the needs of an emerging non-traditional client base.

METHOD

After conducting an extensive literature search for the telephone answering service and call center industries, a synopsis of key differences was developed, along with a call center profile. This provided input for the development of a survey, which would attempt to garner feedback from those who were or would become a call center, contrasted to those who were not and would not become a call center. The result of these endeavor presents a plan for making such a transition.

FINDINGS

The findings of this effort determined that first there were the essential elements which should be present and if lacking must be resolved. Added to that were five items which are common industry dilemmas to be addressed. An inventory of significant call center characteristics was also developed.

Most importantly, areas of focus were advanced. The first was to maintain attention to TSR issues by lengthening training time, increasing training dollars and staffing budgets, coaching, improving retention, enhancing compensation, and implementing telecommuting. Second, was to pursue growth via sales and marketing. Lastly, was to implement key technologies, such as CTI, IVR, ACD, skills-based routing, and workforce management software, along with becoming web-enabled, offering telecommuting, and going virtual.

Turning a Telephone Answering Service into a Call Center

A Dissertation

Presented to the

Faculty of the

School of Business Administration

Kennedy-Western University

In Partial Fulfillment

of the Requirements for the Degree of

Doctor of Philosophy in

Business Administration

by

Peter L. DeHaan

Mattawan, Michigan

TURNING A TELEPHONE ANSWERING SERVICE INTO A CALL CENTER

© 2000

Peter L. DeHaan

CHAPTER 1: TURNING A TELEPHONE ANSWERING SERVICE INTO A CALL CENTER

Introduction

The telephone answering service industry is one which is undergoing rapid changes and a forced evolution. This is due to the combined pressures of the deregulation of the telecommunications industry, ever improving and advancing technology, and low unemployment which is coupled with a shrinking labor force. Once a thriving entrepreneurial, "mom and pop" industry, the closings of bureaus, mergers of companies, and acquisitions by major players have removed some from the industry and forced others to exit. All the while the industry has shrunk, consolidated, and transformed.

Statement of the Problem

By all accounts, the industry is arguably in either the mature or decline phase of its life cycle. Regardless, the end of the traditional telephone answering service industry is likely in sight. What can the industry do to perpetuate itself? For how long will things continue as they once were? What can be done to renew the industry and guide its metamorphosis into a new, different, and better type of business?

With all of these questions and a diversity of possible answers, it is imperative for those within the industry to carefully and methodically consider how to respond to these changing dynamics and the threats they impose.

Industry History

In 1876 Alexander Graham Bell, with the help of his assistant, Thomas Watson, invented the telephone and established the basis for the environment into which the telephone answering service industry would eventually be born. As businesses embraced this new technology, entrepreneurs were given the incentive to capitalize on this communication phenomenon and quickly developed more sophisticated versions of the telephone, as well as switching equipment, long distance service, and other related innovations (DeHaan, 1998).

As more people could make and receive more calls and do so to an ever-expanding list of locations, the need arose to effectively and efficiently handle these calls. In 1917 Genevieve Kidd recognized this need and started the Doctor's Exchange Service in Portland, Oregon. Kidd, a former nurse, saw an opportunity to serve the medical community by providing a service whereby urgent calls could be quickly and effectively handled when the doctor's office was closed. As such, her new business was geared to facilitate the communication needs of doctors, nurses, and dentists. Nine years later she expanded the scope of her growing concern and began serving the business community in a similar fashion. While Kidd was not the only entrepreneur to recognize and capitalize on this need to answer the telephones of others, she is recognized as the first and is largely regarded as the mother of the telephone answering service industry (ATSI, 1989).

Coincident to this, but independently, Pearl Forester took a similar step and opened her answering service in Dallas, Texas in 1918. In like manner, Clark Boyton founded the Physicians and Surgeons Exchange in Philadelphia, Pennsylvania in 1921. Up until this time, the budding industry had no technology available to get their clients' calls to them, so they adopted the concept of "If no answer, call..." The idea was that the medical and business community would publish their answering service's number after their own number, accompanied with the phase, "If no answer, call..." It was Boyton who is credited with the first technological innovation of the industry, when he convinced his telephone company to build a device he called a "stop board," the forerunner of the switchboard. He also persuaded the phone company to run extensions of his client's lines directly to his new device, eliminating the need for "If no answer, call..." as his stop board would allow him to answer his client's lines directly (ATSI, 1989).

Another budding entrepreneur was J. J. Freke-Hayes who in 1923 also conceived the idea of a telephone answering service. Although he was later surprised to learn that the idea had not originated with him, he did go on to advance several other innovative concepts and original ideas. One such initiative, in 1942, was the formation and organization of a meeting of his peers from around the country to discuss issues of common interest. His premise was simple, yet profound, "If I give you a dollar and you give me a dollar – we each have a dollar. But if I give you an idea and you give me an idea, we each have two ideas" (ATSI, 1989). This was the first effort to bring together the independent and disparate members of the growing telephone answering service industry. At the end of the meeting, Freke-Hayes' insight was rewarded when he was elected president of their newly formed group, Associated Telephone Exchanges. This organization was the forerunner to the Associated Telephone Answering Exchanges (ATE) and would later change its name to the Association of Telemessaging Services International (ATSI), which is still in existence today. Because of his insight and innovation, Freke-Hayes has been informally bestowed the title of the father of the telephone answering service industry (ATSI, 1989).

The industry's originating "connection" method of "If no answer, call..." was creative and innovative, as well as simple. Doctor's offices and other businesses would put their own telephone number in their advertisements, on their letterhead and business cards, and in the phone book. Following their own number, they would add the phrase, "If no answer, call ..." followed by a second number. This second number was in fact the number of their telephone answering service. (The concept so pervaded the medical community, that some still use it today, even though technology has long eliminated the necessity of doing so). Although this approach had its elegant simplicity for the client, and was easily understandable to their patients and customers (albeit slightly inconvenient, since a second phone call would need to be made if the first one was not answered), it would become problematic for the answering service as it grew and succeeded. The problem resided in the fact that every caller dialed the same number and there was no way of knowing for which doctor or customer they were calling when the phone rang and was answered. The answering service staff would need to verbally solicit this information from the caller. This was a skill that the answering service staff cultivated and developed, allowing them to subtly obtain the identity of the desired client often without the caller even knowing it. However, as their client base grew it became increasingly difficult to efficiently and effectively determine for whom each caller was calling. Add to this the fact that quite frequently these calls would be placed at a time when the caller was under some degree of distress or concern, causing their own communication to be less than precise or clear. Lastly, simple human error and miscommunication among the staff complicated matters. The end result was that calls would be increasingly given to the wrong doctor simply because the intent of the caller was not, or could not be, correctly discerned or identified (DeHaan, 1998).

As telephone answering services grew and their client base became larger, this problem was exacerbated. Innovative services began to pursue other options, among them, installing an off-premise extension of their client's lines at the answering service. Each extension was then connected to its own telephone. Since each client's line would then be independent of every other client's line, the problem of identifying the doctor or company being called was eliminated. Though this was the primary reason for using off-premise extensions (versus, "If no answer, call..."), there were side benefits as well. With off-premise extensions, a phone call could be answered at either location (that is, the client's office or the answering service). This allowed the answering service to be a back-up for the office, answering phone calls during the day if calls rang too long in the office and handling all calls during lunch or emergencies. Correspondingly, it allowed calls to be answered directly by the client after regular business hours if they chose to do so. Again, as customer bases increased, so did the number of telephones at the answering service. At some locations, the number of phones grew to comical proportions. Lights were connected to the phones' bells so that the ringing phone could be quickly identified and answered. Again, innovation stepped in, and multiple-line phones handling thirty or more lines were installed, replacing vast arrays of single line phones. This too would eventually have its drawbacks and limitations, making way for the next generation of technology. This was the cord-board, capable of having one hundred off-premise extensions connected to it. As the size of telephone answering services grew to more than one hundred lines, additional cord-boards were installed. Many services would grow to have dozens of these devices, sitting side by side, in long rows. Though other ideas, concepts, and approaches would be tried and used, the level of innovation and technology that the cord-board offered would serve the industry well for nearly fifty years, remaining largely unchanged during that time (DeHaan, 1998).

Eventually the venerable cord-board would give way to technology. In the 1950s, entrepreneur and inventor, William Curtin would pioneer technology to advance the industry; though his innovative device would be awarded a patent, he was unable to gain permission to actually use it except in very limited instances. To function, his equipment needed to be physically connected to the telephone network, specially to each client's phone line. Unfortunately, since it was illegal to connect any non-telephone company device to the telephone network, Curtin's invention would languish in obscurity for years. This legal restriction, which had little technical merit, was largely a political one advanced by the dominant and monopolistic AT&T and backed by a supportive FCC. It was not until 1968 and the watershed Carterfone decision that the FCC began, albeit reluctantly, to allow other non-phone company devices to be connected to its network. The guiding premise was that these devices were to not harm the public and had to be beneficial to those using them.

Clearly Curtin's device fit this description, as would the other many ideas he was considering and advancing. Curtin formed a company, Amtelco, to take advantage of this new opportunity. Since he was himself part of the telephone answering service industry, he had the practicality and first-hand insight of an end-user; as such his products were of great interest to the emergent industry. One such significant product was a "line concentrator," which would take up to 100 off-premise extensions and concentrate, or funnel, them down a limited number of "talk-paths," allowing 100 clients to be efficiently serviced. The concentrators could also be placed in other cities. This allowed progressive answering services to expand into new markets and locations while keeping their staff centrally located, which offered the greatest economy-of-scale and optimum management control. Many other manufacturing companies would also make devices for the telephone answering service industry. However, Curtin's Amtelco, with its early start and innovative products, would become and remain the premier equipment provider for the industry (DeHaan, 1998).

The next wave of innovation would occur in the 1980s. A new technology, called DID (Direct-Inward-Dial) service, coupled with call-forwarding, would ultimately pave the way to replace the need for off-premise extensions. Unlike the normal arrangement for telephone service, where every line has a number and every number has a line, DID service foregoes this one to one matching of numbers to lines and instead matches many numbers to a few lines (more technically called trunks). With DID service, many telephone numbers can be routed to a limited number of trunks, in much the same manner as Curtin's concentrator funneled many lines to a few talk paths. Quite simply, the telephone answering service would buy DID service from the phone company, assigning a different number to each client to forward their phone to when they wanted it answered. This allowed the telephone answering service to expand their market even more, since anyone, anywhere, who had call-forwarding could use the service; they no longer needed to be in close proximity to the telephone answering service (off-premise extensions where not cost-effective over long distances). Again, Curtin was to lead the way, designing and manufacturing a small piece of equipment which would allow DID service to be integrated into the thousands of cord boards still in use at the time. Similarly, Curtin upgraded his line concentrator to process DID calls, eventually forming an entire line of products. Other manufactures would pursue similar paths, although Amtelco would remain dominant (DeHaan, 1998).

The mid-eighties witnessed the birth of the personal computer and did much to revolutionize the world as it is now known. Curtin and others had already computerized their products, but each device was, out of necessity, a proprietary platform, using a closed operating system, and employing custom-written and highly specialized software. Now they could begin to integrate personal computer technology into their products, making them more open and less proprietary. Virtually all of today's telephone answering services are computerized. The calls literally ring in on computers, displaying exactly how each particular call should be answered. A computerized version of a message pad, which is customized to the requirements of each client, appears on the computer monitor each time a call is answered. A database holds easily accessible information about the client and also keeps a record of each message, along with substantiation of the subsequent follow-up work that is done. Once messages are in the computer, they can be effortlessly faxed to a client, sent to a text pager, or dispatched over the internet to the client's email. Many of these modern-day systems also contain integrated voice mail, allowing for special announcements to be played to the caller, routine communications to be automatically recorded, or the actual calls to be recorded in their entirety. By the 1990s, this computer revolution resulted in more flexibility, increased innovation, and a greater ability to tap into the rapidly growing array of telephone company services. One such group of services, advanced call forwarding, allowed for calls to be forwarded if they were not answered at the primary location or if the line was busy. Primary-rate interface, integrated services digital network, or PRI-ISDN for short, allows for twenty-three telephone calls to be handled over a single trunk while also providing a data-channel to facilitate computer to computer communication between the answering service and the telephone company; this allows for an unprecedented level of integration, speed, and network efficiency. Automatic number identification, or ANI, an advanced form of caller ID, is available with PRI-ISDN and is utilized by today's modern telephone answering service systems. As the traditional monopoly status of the telephone is further eroded and competition increases, even greater innovation will result (DeHaan, 1998).

Coincident to, and contemporary with, the 1968 Carterfone decision (which set much of this innovation and change in motion) was the introduction of toll-free 800 numbers. Toll-free numbers have allowed telephone answering services to again expand their effective geographic coverage area, literally to all of North America. While many answering services have done so or are doing this, toll-free numbers were also the impetus behind the birth and phenomenal growth of the call center industry, which has emerged since their introduction (Mikol, 1997). The call center industry has since ballooned into a multi-billion dollar a year business (Frost, 1999), greatly dwarfing the older and diminutive telephone answering service industry.

Purpose of Study

The author of this research will be the direct and immediate beneficiary of this effort and the derived results. While there is some value in learning for its own sake and there is some basis for the premise that education is its own reward, the ultimate recipients and beneficiaries of this effort to study, research, and compile relevant information, and the conclusions which result, are organizations in which this author is directly involved.

First is the Company in which this author is president and has an ownership interest. The author's previous research formed much of the basis for the development of the Company's long-range strategic plan, giving shape and overall direction to the business so that it could purposefully and steadfastly move towards the future with the realistic expectation that its existence will be both long-term and successful. Still, that research was incomplete and as such the strategic plan, while a valuable and practical map to the future, was not all it could be. This research will provide the basis on which to revisit and fine-tune the Company's strategic plan, giving more shape and greater form than was previously accomplished.

The second organization which will find benefit from this study is the National Amtelco Equipment Owners Association (NAEO). NAEO is a users' group whose focus is on the products produced by the aforementioned Amtelco. The author is both treasurer and a member of the board of directors for NAEO. The board recently embarked on its own strategic planning project to articulate its desired role in the telephone answering service industry, as well as other markets in which Amtelco equipment is sold. As such, the results of this investigation will likewise assist in that effort.

Third, is the Association of Telemessaging Services International (ATSI). With roots back to J. J. Freke-Hayes' efforts in 1942 to form an answering service organization, ATSI has an ongoing, deep, and long-term record of both serving and being the focal point for all that goes on in the telephone answering service industry. The author is also an ATSI board member. ATSI has undergone fundamental and significant changes in the past year and is currently attempting to reinvent and redefine itself. This report will be able to provide factual direction for that effort, as well as be able to contrast ATSI members' views and perceptions to those of nonmembers. (Only about ten percent of the telephone answering service industry are ATSI members; however, a majority of the non-members are smaller companies and less in tune with the rest of the industry.)

Last, but not least, is that the industry as a whole could benefit from the end results of this research. As this information is published and disseminated, in condensed or summary form, it should provide a basis for discussion and comment, allowing others to be exposed to the prevailing attitudes of those in the industry (at least, the attitudes of those who completed the survey), as well as to be presented with other perspectives and points of view.

Company Overview

The Company was founded in 1960. True to nature of the industry, it was started by a husband-and-wife team who alternated working twelve-hour shifts while the customer base was being established and developed; eventually it was able to sustain the hiring of employees to assist in answering the phones. Like most others at that time, they used a cord-board to answer calls and took messages on paper. Over the years the Company grew, expanded, and made several acquisitions to get to where it is today. With seven locations the Company employs about ninety employees, serves 1,600 clients, and processes over three million calls a year. Today, all work is computerized, with an extensive amount of technology deployed to assist the staff, allowing them the freedom and ability to add the personal touch to an increasingly technologically oriented industry. The Company enjoys the status of the largest and premier service provider in thirteen of sixteen primary markets it serves.

The Company, and its leaders, are recognized throughout the industry, pioneering new and innovative ways of conducting business and serving clients. The Company was an early adopter of Amtelco equipment and has seen the benefits from doing so. The founder of the Company served on the ATSI board of directors and ascended to the presidency of that organization in the mid-eighties. The chairman of the board likewise served on the ATSI board of directors and was a founding member and the first president of NAEO. As already mentioned, the president of the Company has followed this tradition and currently serves on the board of directors for both ATSI and NAEO. The company's general manager is a leading board member for the Professional Inbound Network (PIN), another industry user group, which is pointing the way towards the call center industry. In the past, the Company has been represented in several other industry groups, including the Michigan Telemessaging Association (MTA), the Great Lakes TeleServices Association (GLTSA), and the Cad Com Equipment Owners (CEO) user group. Whether serving as association leaders, speaking at conventions, or writing industry articles, the Company has been a visible and active industry force.

User Group Overview

The users' group, NAEO, was founded in 1984 out of a direct need and desire to support Amtelco in the ongoing development and enhancement of arguably the most revolutionary system ever developed for the industry. This system, the Electronic Video Exchange (EVE), was the industry's first significant computerized system and set the stage, as well as the bar, for all that followed. As with all innovation, EVE was not without its glitches and NAEO was formed, in part, to work with Amtelco to stabilize the platform and move the product forward. Over the years, NAEO has grown and expanded, producing a string of valuable and helpful products for its members. Currently NAEO is the most successful and largest of the industry users' group and is well positioned should it elect to expand further.

Association Overview

As previously mentioned, the Association of Telemessaging Services International (ATSI) traces its beginnings to 1942. It grew steadily over the years and in 1988 boasted almost 1050 members (ATSI, 1989). Ten years later its membership has dwindled to a fraction of that. The consolidation of the industry has taken a huge toll on the membership numbers of ATSI. To address this problem, ATSI announced that the call center association, ATA (American Teleservices Association) would begin providing management services to ATSI in 1999, with an eye toward merger, in which ATSI would become a subset of ATA, one year later. At the last minute, ATA withdrew its management offer and put the merger possibility on indefinite hold; they cited an immediate and pressing need to restructure internally.

Although ATSI members seemed to view an ATA merger as unavoidable and an inevitable conclusion, they breathed a collective sigh of relief when the deal was cancelled. They had already begun to lament the fact that ATSI was going away and now that a reprieve was given, a renewed enthusiasm and vigor surfaced, this added to the momentum to give ATSI another try and to make it work. Under the present leadership and tireless dedication of ATSI president Raymond Baggerly, the tide has turned and there is renewed interest in an effort to keep ATSI viable.

About the Author

The author started in the industry in 1979. With a technical background and FCC license, he began work as a technician in the company's pager division (which was later sold, allowing for more focus on the telephone answering division). At that time, AT&T provided one-stop shopping for all aspects of the technical needs of the telephone answering service. AT&T leased the cord-boards, maintained them as needed, made the requisite connections of the off-premise extensions, and repaired the lines when they malfunctioned. As such, there was no need for any involvement of the technical staff with the telephone answering service division.

That all changed with the installation of the EVE system (a non-AT&T provided piece of equipment) and the near simultaneous forced divestiture of AT&T. Suddenly there was an immediate and significant technical need in the telephone answering service; the author assumed this role. A year later he joined Amtelco as manager of their service department. During his tenure there he also worked as a programmer, writing computer code for the next generation of the EVE system, as well as a technical writer, designing several technical manuals.

In 1988 the author returned to his former company as the Special Projects Manager and was later promoted to General Manager. In 1990, he completed work on his Bachelors degree, researching and writing his Bachelors thesis which was titled, "Hiring and Retention for the Telephone Answering Service." Another significant step occurred in 1995. He was promoted to president and also became a stockholder when the company doubled its size as a result of an acquisition. In 1998, he completed work on his Masters degree and copyrighted his Masters' thesis, "The Telephone Answering Service Industry: Preparing for the Future."

During his tenure in the industry, the author has made several presentations before industry groups, including ATSI, NAEO, PIN, MTA, GLTSA, and CEO. He has written dozens of articles about the industry on a vast array of technical and management issues. He has served on the board of directors for MTA and is currently a board member for both NAEO and ATSI.

Importance of Study

The telephone answering service industry is considered, at best, to be a mature industry or, at worst, a declining industry. In a mature industry, few new clients are found and those who are added, merely replace those who leave. To compound matters, sales are often made at the expense of a competitor, as accounts are merely traded back and forth;

in essence it is a zero-sum game. Even less optimistic is the outlook in a declining industry. Here the new sales are not sufficient to replace lost business. Businesses must tighten their belt as their revenue stream contracts; eventually some are bought out, while others close their doors. In either case, there is great cause for concern as days of growth and virtually assured success are past (DeHaan, 1998).

This industry consolidation is confirmed by ATSI, which put the number of industry players at 10,000 in 1988, dropping to 5,000 by 1998 (ATSI, 1989). It is speculated that there are much less than 4,000 today.

Given this as a backdrop, it is imperative to formulate a plan to either reinvent the industry or to migrate it to the next level. The author's previous research proposed the former, while this work will address the latter.

Although either reinventing oneself or moving to a different industry are viable, acceptable, and pragmatic steps for a company to take, it is this author's belief that the first approach is a necessary short-term step while the second alternative is the required, ideal long-term tactic.

Therefore, one could conclude that this research, along with other progressive, "out-of-the-box" thinking, is needed if the industry players are to survive. Ultimately, it will be up to each company and each organization to consider this research and its conclusions, making informed decisions on how to best prepare for the future.

Scope of Study

Earlier research by this author in 1998 advanced several ideas and recommendations. These were merged into a cohesive plan of action to extend the life of the telephone answering service industry in general and specifically in this author's company. In many respects these recommended initiatives were pointing at and moving towards the call center industry. While the implementation of these suggestions will likely forestall the predicted demise of the telephone answer service industry, they will also likely be equally unable to allow it to continue long term into the foreseeable future.

Rationale of Study

In addition to proposing a path to the future, this previous research also pointed out the need for additional study, investigation, and exploration. It is the intent of this dissertation to do just that, by more carefully considering how the telephone answering service industry (or at least its more progressive, far-thinking members) can successfully and effectively navigate the transition into becoming a call center.

Limitations of Study

It is unrealistic and ill-advised to expect that any research effort, no matter how noble or rigorously pursued, will be complete, all-encompassing, without error, and devoid of bias. This endeavor is no exception.

First, take into account the authors of the literature which was considered and will be reported in the literature search in the next chapter. It is unknown how thorough, meticulous, and fair these individuals were in producing their work. Could their work be the result of a preconceived bias or a hidden agenda? Could they merely be echoing the errors of previous authors? It has been said that a lie repeated often enough is soon accepted as fact. Though this author will attempt to avoid the perpetuation of misinformation and propaganda, the very attempt to do so introduces the author's own judgement and perceptions into the equation.

Next, one should consider those who take part in the survey. It is not determinable how much the opinions of those who are not predisposed to take surveys differ from those who are so inclined. Will this unknown variable skew the results of this survey and if so, how much and in which direction? The degree to which respondents consider a question before answering it is another limitation. Do they carefully consider each answer or quickly select what first comes to mind? Regardless, which approach produces better and more accurate results? Also, consider that some respondents may not read or correctly understand the survey's instructions, rendering their responses questionable. Then, there is the issue of how to deal with incomplete surveys. Does one eliminate the entire survey, only the incomplete section, or make the best use of whatever information is provided? Again, regardless of how one elects to proceed, any course of action will impact the results.

Then there is the survey itself. Any survey, no matter how well designed, must make several trade-offs. These include the survey's comprehensiveness versus the time required for completion, providing too much incentive to submit it contrasted to no inducement at all, and keeping dissemination costs down yet making it easy to obtain. All of these issues influence the design of the survey, determine the target group's propensity to complete and return it, and impact the seriousness in which it is considered.

Lastly, consider the limitations of this author. While possessing a wealth of industry knowledge and experience, it is essentially insider knowledge and experience. It is, therefore, conceivable that his personal history could form the basis for a presumption which might obscure him from realizing relevant trends, seeing significant options, or considering radical alternatives. Any biases or preconceived notions which the author possesses will undoubtedly worm their way into his work, despite his best efforts to avoid its occurrence and to remain open-minded. Succinctly, and to the point, this effort will only produce the results which the author will allow it to.

Definition of Terms

24 x 7: A notation to indicate continuous operations, twenty-four hours a day, seven days a week.

ACD: An acronym for Automatic Call Distribution; it is a method of routing the longest waiting call to the next (or most) available TSR.

Agent: Another name for TSR.

ANI (Automatic Number Identification): A service offered by the telephone company to call centers and other telecommunication companies, which provides the number of the calling party (and sometimes their name) electronically to the called party while the phone is ringing. Comparable to caller-ID, the analogous residential service.

Answering service: See, "telephone answering service."

ATE: Associated Telephone Answering Exchanges, an early association of the telephone answering service industry.

ATSI: Association of Telemessaging Services International, the voice of the telephone answering service industry.

Benchmarking: A statistical procedure of gathering key industry parameters, which are presented as averages, means, and sometimes modes, along with high and low values to provide typical performance metrics. This process allows an organization to compare and contrast their numbers with established industry results.

Bureau: Another name for a telephone answering service or call center.

Call center: A term which refers to a telemarketing operation. A call center can specialize in outbound calls (where the call center places sales calls), inbound calls (where consumers call to place orders or obtain information), or both.

Caller: A customer, or potential customer, of a client of a telephone answering service or call center. The primary interaction of a Telephone Service Representative is actually with their clients' customers and not so much as with the clients themselves.

Carterfone decision: A historical turning point in telecommunications history, which established the environment for competition, new and innovative services, and ultimately the deregulation of the entire industry.

CEO: An industry user group, Cad Com Equipment Owners.

Client: A customer of a telephone answering service or call center.

Coaching: A method of improving customer service, whereby a trained mentor provides one-on-one feedback and encouragement to TSRs through a process of ongoing self-discovery.

Contact-enabled web site: A web site which is able to integrate with a call center, specifically a web-enabled call center, in order to provide various methods of interaction, including listing toll free numbers to talk with a TSR, fax numbers, email addresses, call-back buttons, talk-to-me buttons, and internet chat options.

Cord-board: An electromechanical device first used to manually switch telephone calls and later adapted by the pioneers of the telephone answering service industry as an effective means of answering their clients' lines.

CTI (Computer-Telephony Integration): The integration of a computer system with a telephone switch in order to allow relevant computer database information about the caller or account to be presented to the TSR simultaneously with the call itself.

Inbound telemarketing: One of two aspects of telemarketing where customers or prospects call a company for assistance when they want or need it, as opposed to outbound telemarketing where the company calls customers or prospects. Inbound telemarketing is a reactive process and non-intrusive.

Internet: An international network of networks, allowing email and information to be readily sent from one computer to another.

ISDN (Integrated Services Digital Network): An international standard for digital telephony communications.

Live: A somewhat inane term to indicate that a call will be processed by a real person as opposed to automation from a voice mail system or an answering machine. The main benefit of a telephone answering service or call center is that it provides "live" interaction with the caller.

Metrics: The gathering and study of quantifiable data industry or organizational data; used in benchmarking.

NAEO: An industry user group, the National Amtelco Equipment Owners.

Off-premise extension (OPX): A telephone company service whereby an extension of a telephone line is connected to a second location. This was at one time commonly used by telephone answering services to answer their clients' telephones.

Outbound telemarketing: One of two aspects of telemarketing whereby a company proactively calls consumers or businesses in order to make sales. This is the subset of telemarketing which is intrusive and therefore receives a great deal of negative press. Contrast to "inbound telemarketing."

Outsourcing: The concept of transferring internal company functions to an external organization. Outsourcing is done to save money, improve quality, and/or free company resources for other activities. Outsourcing was first done in the data-processing industry and has spread to areas, including telephone answering services, call centers, and telemarketing firms.

PIN: An acronym for Personal Identification Number; most telephone answering services assign to and reference their clients by a PIN. Also, PIN is an industry user group: Professional Inbound Network.

PRI-ISDN (Primary-rate interface ISDN): A high capacity version of ISDN which allows for twenty-three simultaneous conversions. See, "ISDN."

Push: In a web-enabled call center, the ability of an agent or TSR to take control of the customer's internet browser and send them to various web sites or pages on a web site. This is useful when a web surfer cannot find what he is looking for and contacts the call center for assistance.

Quality Monitoring: The random and periodic act of listening to TSRs' phone calls for the purpose of evaluation, training, education, and/or assuring compliance to instructions and policies. Though TSRs are made aware that they will be monitored in the course of performing their work, most organizations do not notify TSRs as to when the monitoring will occur.

Queue: A "stack" of calls on hold (or ringing) and waiting to be answered. Many telephone answering services and most inbound call centers make use of a queue for increased efficiency, greater productivity, and overall shorter waiting times for callers. A queue is analogous to waiting in line at a supermarket checkout or an amusement park ride.

Rep. (Representative): Another name for TSR.

Screen pop: In CTI (Computer-Telephony Integration) applications, causing a computer to display information about the call at the same time as the TSR answers the call. See, "CTI."

Self-service: Designing a web site so that customers can access information about products, prices, orders, shipments, invoices, and other records, thereby allowing them to obtain needed information without human intervention.

Service Level: Measurements which are indicative of the efficiency with which calls are processed. A common service level parameter is the speed in which calls are answered; the oft quoted, but unsubstantiated, value of this metric is to answer eighty percent of the calls within twenty seconds.

Surfer: A potential customer who is viewing one's web site, often in an unintentional or haphazard manner.

TAS: An acronym for telephone answering service.

Talk path: A pair of wires over which a telephone conversion can take place, typically connecting two telephone systems together. Amtelco's line concentrator used talk paths to connect callers to another system, allowing them to be answered.

Talk time: The amount of time a TSR spends talking with a caller. Compare to "total time" and wrap-up" time.

Telecommuting: The act of using computer and telecommunication technology to perform one's job from a remote location, typically from a home office.

Telemarketing: Sales and marketing conducted using the telephone. It is classified as inbound or outbound. See, "inbound telemarketing" and "outbound telemarketing."

Telephone answering service (answering service): A company which provides a service whereby a client's phone is answered, a message is taken or information provided to the caller, and the results documented and dispatched to the client.

Telephony: A term used to refer to telephone lines, trunks, circuits, related equipment, and the information (voice, fax, data, etc.) which is transmitted over them.

Total time: The total amount of time a TSR spends serving a caller. Total time is the sum of "talk time" and "wrap-up time."

TSR: An acronym for Telephone Service Representative and generically refers to the employees who use the telephone to serve callers. It is a term commonly used in the telemarketing and call center industries and somewhat in the telephone answering service industry. Other labels include, "agent," "rep.," and "operator."

Trunk: A connection path linking two telephone switches, generally this is between two telephone company central offices or between a central office and the end-user's equipment.

Web: A commonly used designation for the World Wide Web (or WWW). It is not the internet, but a subset of it whereby graphical images and information can be viewed remotely by other individuals.

Web-enabled Call Center: A call center which is capable of handling a variety of contact methods from Web sites, including phone calls, faxes, email, call-back requests, talk-to-me requests, and internet chat.

Wrap-up time: The time that a TSR spends to complete the work on a call, after the caller has hung-up. Depending on the type of call, wrap-up time can last from only a few seconds to several minutes.

Overview of Study

The results of this study have the potential to impact all those who are willing to consider it. To the Company it will provide much needed information to fine-tune an existing strategic plan, offering additional guidance and direction, while presenting an enlightened and efficient path to the future. To the user group (NAEO), it will provide an important snapshot of the industry as a whole, allowing this to be compared and contrasted with its own members and providing a critical view from outside of the organization. To the association (ATSI), it will provide insight into the fears and concerns members, and non-members alike, have toward the future, allowing the association to take proactive steps to confront those concerns and meet needs not yet addressed. Lastly, to the industry as a whole, this study will provide each constituent with one more item to consider as they plan for their organization's future.

While it would be naïve and presumptuous to assume that the future of an entire industry rests on the results of this body of work, it is accurate to state that the industry's future is certainly not assured and is in question. This research will provide clarity, direction, and guidance to an industry in need and, along with the ideas and influences of others, help to shape the future, assisting the telephone answering service industry, and its members, to make it be a good and successful one. Toward that end, this author is committed.

CHAPTER 2: REVIEW OF THE LITERATURE

Introduction

The focus of the literature search was on the two topics found in the title of this dissertation: telephone answering services and call centers. One variation of each topic was also included. Each industry has attempted to redefine both their form and their scope by advancing new and thought-provoking labels. This does not imply that new industries are being birthed, but rather that new perspectives are being introduced into existing configurations.

For the telephone answering service industry, this redefinition has spawned the label of telemessaging or teleservices, while the call center industry is seeing its clarification in the broadening concept of a contact center (along with many variants). Though all four are arguably a matter of semantics and some would even elect to use them interchangeably, depending on the situation, there are differences. Not only will the differences of these industries be documented and delineated as a result of the literature search, but also their commonalties.

While a great deal of information could be found about call centers and contact centers, both in the form of books and especially periodicals, there was precious little to be uncovered about telephone answering services and telemessaging services. While conducting this author's previous research in 1998, some information was garnered about telephone answering services from two industry periodicals, a smattering of web sites, and one trade group newsletter; no books could be found on the subject. Since that time, little has been added to this small compilation of data. In fact, the industry's premier publication, *Answer* magazine, languished through the latter part of 1998 and beginning of 1999, eventually publishing its final issue, with little fanfare, in June of that year. This left one other industry publication, *Connections Magazine*, as the only remaining voice of the industry. Sadly, the last two years of articles in *Connections Magazine* had no content relevant for this literature search.

Telephone Answering Service and Telemessaging

The result of this portion of the literature search is contained in three resources. The first two are the 1989 *Answer* magazine article entitled "TAS History" and the results of ATSI's 1998 survey, labeled "ATSI Statistical Survey: Final Results." The final source resides in this author's own 1998 work, "The Telephone Answering Service Industry: Preparing for the Future."

Although no longer containing current industry information, the 1989 ATSI article in *Answer* magazine, "TAS History," does at least provide a snapshot of the quantitative condition of the industry at that point in time. It stated that ATSI had "nearly 1050 members in 1988," and that those members represented about sixty percent of the industry capacity. It estimated that industry wide there were over one million clients using telephone answering services. It added that "the telephone will be put to greater use in the days to come," implying that this would positively impact the number of clients needing the industry's assistance (ATSI, 1989, p. 34).

Additionally, the industry employed over forty thousand employees to appropriately serve those one million clients. Collectively, these million clients generated, and forty thousand employees answered and processed, 850 million calls a year. Again, the projection was made that this number would increase over time as businesses grew and changed. Lastly, the annual billing for the telephone answering service industry was put at $800 million (ATSI, 1989). These numbers are summarized in Table 1. It should be noted that these are all estimates, projections, and interpolations, as there is no industry-wide reporting mechanism.

Table 1: <u>Summary of Telephone Answering Service Data (1988)</u>

Item	Quantity
Number of ATSI members	1050
Market share for ATSI members	60%
Number of people employed (industry wide)	40,000
Number of clients served (industry wide)	1,000,000
Number of calls processed annually (industry wide)	850,000,000
Annual billing (industry wide)	$800,000,000

More recent figures, as of 1995, and proclaimed by industry insider Steve Michaels, projected the total industry billing to have increased to $2.4 billion. This is a 173% increase over the eight-year period, averaging out to fifteen percent a year. This is not to imply that the average industry business grew at that rate, but rather the industry as a whole grew at that rate. Also, during this same time frame, the number of industry players decreased by 2.4% (DeHaan, 1998). No other industry data could be located. (This data will be later contrasted with similar data from the call center industry.)

In 1997, ATSI conducted a member survey to compile statistical data about their membership. This data was aggregated and presented to members at the 1998 annual convention. It should be noted that seventy-seven members responded out of about five hundred, for a fifteen percent response rate. This, however, needs to be put into the context of an industry estimated to be at about four thousand. (Only those items relevant to this study will be summarized.)

In assessing the annual revenues of the members' businesses, forty-nine percent placed themselves in the category of $350 thousand to one million. Roughly one fourth of the respondents were above that range and one fourth below that range (ATSI, 1998). This tracks with an analysis of Michaels' figures which pegged annual average revenue at $585,000 in 1995 (DeHaan, 1998). When projecting revenue trends, sixty-five percent said that their revenue was growing, twenty percent declared theirs to be stable, and only fourteen percent affirmed a declining revenue stream (ATSI, 1998).

In a similar vein, the trend of their number of clients served was also measured. Here the results were not as positive as the revenue trends, though they are nonetheless pointing upwards. Forty-two percent said their number of clients was increasing; thirty-one percent said stable; and twenty-six percent, declining (ATSI, 1998). These are shown below in Table 2.

Table 2: Telephone Answering Service Growth Trends (1998)

Status	Revenue	Number of Clients
Growing	65%	42%
Stable	20%	31%
Declining	14%	26%
Totals	99%	99%

Note: Totals do not equal 100% due to rounding.

Contrasting these two trends for revenue and number of clients, it can be seen that revenue tendencies are more robust than client base growth, suggesting that revenue gains are not all tied to an increasing client base. In fact, for both sets of numbers to correctly coexist, some who have experienced negative changes in their client base had to have seen stability or improvement in their revenues. Correspondingly, some who experienced no change in their client base must have likewise enjoyed revenue improvements.

These facts, however, run contrary to the widespread conclusion of this author's previous literature search which documented that industry players have suffered from both diminishing client bases and constricting revenue streams (DeHaan 1998). However, this discrepancy could be attributed to one of three items. First, the people who completed the survey were all ATSI members and even though ATSI is the voice of the industry its members are not representative of the industry. Second, those who had better than average results in the industry could have had a greater propensity to complete and return their surveys. Lastly, those who completed the surveys may have had a tendency to put a positive spin on their answers. Regardless, the survey results should not be thought of as contradictory to this author's previous research, rather they should be viewed as complementary perspectives, being two sides of the same coin.

Of those answering services represented in the surveys, eighty-one percent had been in existence fifteen years or more. Only six percent had a tenure of less than seven years and only one respondent had been in business less than two years (ATSI, 1998).

Two other noteworthy items were charted in the survey. The first was a glimpse into the number of services which were attempting to gain national clients, expanding beyond their own local market, along with their success at doing so. This is interpreted by the percentage of their client base using toll-free numbers versus local numbers. Thirty-six percent had no clients using toll-free numbers and forty-seven percent had less than ten percent. Only fifteen percent had between ten and forty percent; while no one had more than forty percent (ATSI, 1998).

The second item of significance was the percentage of revenue which the respondents enjoyed from enhanced services accounts, that is accounts which transcend the traditional taking and processing of a message. Here the results were somewhat more encouraging. While twenty-one percent did none of this type of business, a full fifty-three percent of respondents enjoyed up to ten percent of their revenue from these non-traditional sources. Twenty-three percent were grouped in the ten to forty percent ranges; again no one was over the forty percent mark (ATSI, 1998). Both of these represented movement into areas which were virtually none-existent in the telephone answering service industry ten years ago and exemplify forays into areas more closely associated with call centers than with telephone answering services. Table 3 provides side-by-side detail from both of these service migration trends. These developments work in tandem, since much of the enhanced services are in fact provided over toll-free numbers. (This is not to imply that telephone answering service is not provided using toll-free numbers, nor that enhanced service clients do not use toll numbers.) This tracks with one of this author's recommendations for the industry in 1998, that "the pragmatic approach would be to expand into order-taking and then re-evaluate the situation ... to move to embrace the greater call center industry" (DeHaan, 1998).

Table 3: <u>Noteworthy Service Trends (1998)</u>

Percent	Using Toll-Free Numbers	Revenue from Enhanced Services
None	36%	21%
Less than 10 percent	47%	53%
10 to 20 percent	12%	15%
20 to 30 percent	1%	5%
30 to 40 percent	3%	3%
More that 40 percent	0%	0%
<u>No response</u>	<u>1%</u>	<u>3%</u>
Total	100%	100%

Also covered in the survey were pay rates for the front-line staff, the telephone service representatives (TSRs). Informal discussions among answering service owners and managers place the expenses attributable to TSR staff at thirty to fifty percent of total expenses. This makes the hourly TSR wage a significant variable in the profit equation. Three wage-related questions were included in the survey. The average TSR starting wage was determined to be $6.62 an hour; the average hourly rate for all TSRs was $8.24 an hour; and the average loaded (including taxes and benefits) payroll cost for all TSRs was $10.03 an hour (ATSI, 1998); these median results are shown in Table 4.

Table 4: Median Hourly Rates for Telephone Service Representatives (1998)

Category	Hourly Rate
Starting Hourly Rate	$6.62
Average Hourly Rate	$8.24
Average Loaded Hourly Rate	$10.03

Lastly, some metrics were obtained to determine a benchmark for some common industry service level indicators such as speed to answer, hold parameters, length of call, and productivity. First, among those surveyed, the average time it took to answer a call was pegged at fourteen seconds; this is roughly two and a half rings (a ring is six seconds). Once the call was answered, seventy-nine percent were not put on hold, leaving only twenty-one percent who experienced any hold time. Of this twenty-one percent who were placed on hold, the average length of time on hold was twenty-nine seconds. The actual length of the calls (minus hold time) averaged out to forty-nine seconds. Lastly, the occupancy rate, which is the percentage of time that TSRs are processing calls, versus waiting for calls was forty-seven percent (ATSI, 1998). These five standards for service level are summarized in Table 5.

Table 5: Telephone Answering Service Level Metrics (1998)

Category	Median
Wait time before answer	14 seconds (2.3 rings)
Calls placed on hold	21%
Hold time when placed on hold	29 seconds
Time per call (sans hold time)	49 seconds
Occupancy Rate	47%

The extensive literature search conducted in 1998 by DeHaan allowed a composite view of the telephone answering service industry to be painted. First, it was a fragmented industry with a limited number of constituents taking part in the various formal groups existing within it (pp. 22-23). Although classified as a mature industry (p. 27), its revenue was increasing at a rate of twelve percent to fifteen percent annually (pp. 23, 31) and expected to "surpass the three billion dollar mark by year 2000" (p. 23). At the same time, the number of players in the industry was decreasing at a "dramatic" rate (p. 35). Adding to the confusion were the divergent assertions that the industry was making a rebound (p. 35) and that "the telephone service industry is not going away," (p. 42).

The industry's current environment is shaped by the twin forces of the deregulation of the telephone industry and pervasive influence of the personal computer (p. 26), opening the way for an unlimited array of choices (p. 25), the chief of which was becoming a call center (p. 27). To do this, the industry needs to continuously re-educate themselves and become cognizant of the many technological alternatives potential clients have to the industry's services (pp. 24, 38), harnessing much of this same technology to make it past the crossroads it faces (p.25). Voice mail technology, once viewed as a threat to the industry, was experiencing a public backlash, pointing the way back towards live telephone answering service (p. 38). Added to this was the industry's embrace of the general business trend of consolidations and mergers (pp. 32, 35) along with a sudden interest from outside the industry for investment (pp. 33, 36) and the result was an industry in the midst of upheaval (DeHaan, 1998).

The primary strength of the industry was documented as the human element, which should be viewed as its main competitive advantage. A second strength was twenty-four hours a day, 365 days a year staffing availability (DeHaan, 1998, pp. 38, 49). On the other hand, industry weaknesses were identified as poor sales and marketing efforts (p.42), possessing little collateral for financing (p. 31), not charging enough for the service provided (pp. 28, 46), and its status as a mature industry (p. 26).

Industry threats included new technology and the negative public perception that it does little more than take messages (DeHaan, 1998, p. 24). Conversely opportunities for the industry included inexpensive technology, especially personal computers (p. 24), the opportunity to easily migrate towards order-taking (p. 27), the general business trend towards outsourcing (p. 43), and open architecture systems which provide greater flexibility, creativity, and end-user control (p. 44).

The survey, which followed the literature search, performed a SWOT (strengths, weaknesses, opportunities, and threats) analysis and confirmed several of the above findings, in addition to adding new ones. Evaluating the industry's strengths and weaknesses was an internal look at the industry. Correspondingly, it was the external environment which presented the opportunities and threats that the industry must consider and address (DeHaan, 1998).

According to the survey, the industry's five greatest strengths were its flexibility in meeting client requests, the TSR staff (that is, the provision of "live" service), the existing technology infrastructure in place in their offices, having a focus on the needs and concerns of clients, and being staffed twenty-four hours-a-day, seven days-a-week (also referred to as 24 x 7) (DeHaan, 1998, pp. 120-122). The complete list of industry strengths is included in Appendix A.

On the other hand, the five most often mentioned industry weaknesses were not charging enough for their services, having a lack of adequate management skills, inability to successfully promote and market their services, possessing a reputation for providing poor service, and not possessing enough technological knowledge or infrastructure (DeHaan, 1998, pp. 122-125). All of the industry weaknesses are detailed in Appendix B.

When looking at the external environment, the top five industry opportunities were the benefits that new technology could offer, the prospect of providing telephone order-taking services, the vast potential of the internet (to serve clients, market services, and develop new services), developing niche markets, and providing one-stop-shopping to clients. Notice that the last two items, niche markets and one-stop-shopping, are mutually exclusive opportunities; only one of the two can be pursued. These, along with the remaining industry opportunities are included in Appendix C. Interestingly, of all the opportunities which were identified, fully fifty-one percent of the responses fit into the category of opportunities for new services. While all are worth considering, the top four received significant mention. They are telephone order-taking, internet services, help desk services, and customer service lines. Breaking these new service opportunities down further, to form another sub-set, fully half of the responses fit the description of call center services (DeHaan, 1998, pp. 126-133).

Alternatively, when industry threats were considered, the one most oft mentioned was competitive forces from alternate technologies. Next, was labor pressures; followed by automation, technology, and being unprofessional (actually this should properly be classified as a threat, but the respondents choose not to view it as such) (DeHaan, 1998, pp. 133-135). Appendix D contains the complete list of industry threats.

Lastly, a concluding question asked for recommendations on how to proceed in the future. The number one category was to acquire and use technology; followed by improve staffing (hiring and training practices, as well as compensation). Five responses tied for third; they were increase knowledge, pursue niche markets, provide superior customer service, and diversify (DeHaan, 1998, pp. 138-142). It was noted, with some irony, that technology was considered to be both a major strength and weakness, as well as a both a major opportunity and threat, and was prominently included among the list of recommendations. Clearly, it can be concluded that technology will play a prominent role in the future of the telephone answering service industry.

DeHaan (1998) completed his thesis by advancing several recommendations for the industry. These were based on an analysis of the recommendations uncovered in the literature search and documented in the industry survey. Though there were a total of fifteen recommendations, three major initiatives were identified. They were to diversify into telephone order-taking, pursue internet opportunities, and invest in technology (p. 168). All fifteen recommendations are detailed in Appendix E.

Call Centers

"The definition of an actual call center appears to be a moving target," states Alessandra Bianchi (1998, p. 38). "No one really agrees on what a call center is," adds Brad Cleveland. If anyone should know it would be Cleveland, who is President of the industry consulting firm Incoming Call Center Management. Because call centers can span multiple sites, they are not properly termed a "center" and, he notes wryly, they also process more than just calls (Bianchi, 1998, p. 38). In times past, customers were won and retained via personal, face-to-face meetings, but today these relationships are increasingly "being defined by telephone transactions," (Tamar, 1996, p. 24). In fact, according to estimates, a whopping seventy-five percent of all business interactions with customers are being conducted by call centers (Elwell, 1999). This dramatic change has caught the attention of corporate America, who are getting involved with the call center business (Tehrani, 1997). Their interest in call centers revolves around a desire to provide a "better, more personalize service," (Read, 1998, p. 28). "For many enterprises," notes Brian Riggs and Mary Thyfault, "a call center provides the first – and sometimes only – direct contact with customers," (1999, p. 53). With every phone call, there exists an opportunity to make an impression; it can be a good one or a bad one. Each phone call is a chance to keep a customer or lose a customer; to sell more or sell less. It is no longer a call center but rather a "vital hub for creating and maintaining profitable relationships," adds Ron Elwell. "It's no wonder that the call center's role has evolved from simply handling calls to managing customer exceptions," (1999, p. 60). IBM's Patricia Mitchell is even more emphatic, identifying call centers as "the single greatest source of competitive advantage [in] successfully establishing and maintaining customer relationships," (1998, pp. 64-66).

It should be noted that there are actually two types of call center activity, the proactive, outbound telemarketing and the reactive, 800 number, inbound endeavor. Of course, some call centers perform both types of activity. Although sometimes it is unclear which version of a call center is being discussed in any given circumstance, it is the inbound call center which is the focus of this study and provides the most logical migration path for the telephone answering service industry. Therefore, this review disregarded information explicitly about outbound call centers and reported on inbound call centers to the extent it was feasible.

When considering inbound call centers, it was noted that their attentiveness is on building "customer satisfaction, loyalty, retention, and ultimately higher profitability," stated Mitchell. They need to be "service oriented ... with robust processes, state-of-the art technology and highly trained agents," (1998, p. 66). As these factors merge and succeed, even greater expectations "are being heaped on the call center to be a customer loyalty enabler, a competitive weapon, and ultimately, a profit center," (Anderson & Taylor, 1998, p. 84). In regard to turning a call center into a profit center, Peter Theis offered three ideas. First, was the oft-mentioned goal of developing positive and long-term relationships with customers. The second idea was data collection for the purpose of influencing "marketing strategies and product mix." Lastly, he built a case for the value of call centers doing market research "live," as to eliminate the barriers of automated computers or confusing written surveys, by conducting the survey using "natural language" over the telephone (Theis, 1999a, p. 17).

This is a far different picture than what exists in the minds of many consumers (although arguably this was mostly a result of outbound call center activity). Jeremy James acknowledged that many people view call centers "as the sweat shops of the 20th century" (Slater, 1999, p. 56). This perspective was not surprising given that the model for call centers was, in fact, the assembly line from the industrial age, advocating narrowly defined jobs which were preformed repeatedly for the quickest results and greatest efficiency (Wood, 1997). The goal had been to handle as many calls, as quickly as possible, with a limited number of TSRs. This resulted in low morale and high turnover (Slater, 1999). The end result of this approach was that TSRs were pushed to do more, both by their employer and the callers, and to do it faster and faster (Tamer, 1996).

Thomas Cook acknowledged the error of that mentality, "We have changed our thinking from 'cost of agent' to 'value of service to customer'" (Slater, 1999, p. 56). Slater added, "Customer service equals customer loyalty equals money," (1999, p. 56). As such, many industries, which never considered call centers in the past are now utilizing them. In doing so, it was as likely that their objective was to reduce costs as it was to increase revenue (Bianchi, 1998). Viewing call centers as profit centers, in this way, led to a new call center paradigm that quality was as important, or more so, than the quantity of calls processed (Kahn, 1999). Executives in widely varying industries increasingly recognized that providing excellent customer service in their call centers was, and will be, critical in both retaining existing customers, as well as in obtaining new ones (Riggs & Thyfault, 1999). With this as a push from the top down, it was no wonder that managers began increasingly looking to quality as being "the competitive differentiator in the call center" (Tamer, 1996, p. 24). Towards that end, *TeleProfessional* magazine conducted an audit of more than one hundred call centers to quantify and rank various call center attributes, such as technology, service offerings, monitoring capabilities, project exclusivity, and center size. However, conspicuously missing from this list was quality. Sadly, they admitted, one "can't quantify quality" (Karr, 1998b, p. 60). However, in a later issue, it was stated that "defining and measuring success [is] more critical and difficult than ever before" (Mandaro, 1999, p. 55). In today's competitive, consumer-driven marketplace, customer loyalty is only a phone call away from being lost. The goal of the call center manager must be to provide each caller with a compelling reason to call back the next time they are in need, rather than to call a competitor. Quality of service was the single most significant differentiator in dealing with customers' growing expectations. The manager of the future will need to place even greater emphasis on quality in order to be successful (Reiners, 1999).

MCI's Kevin Burns states that one of the main driving forces for call center growth is the concept of mass customization. Mass customization advocates that each customer should be treated differently as opposed to having a one-size-fits-all mentality. The premise of mass customization is not without its detractors, as it involves gathering as much information about customers as possible. This allows each and every customer interaction to be as focused as possible for the greatest chance of success. Call centers are uniquely positioned to both collect and utilize mass customization data (MCI, 1997). This opinion was reiterated by Derek Slater who said that service can be personalized when companies collect "increasing amounts of information about their customers," (Slater, 1999, p. 60). He continued that the fundamental premise for this effort is the belief that the more a company knows about individual customers, the better they will be served. Consequently, since customers will stick with the company which knows them best, the more loyal these customers will become.

However, he did concede that this knowledge came at a price, for "the call center's hard-won efficiency" took a "productivity hit" as this information was gathered and recorded. Still, he deemed the effort, and anticipated results, to be a worthwhile trade-off (Slater, 1999, p. 60).

Call Center Facts

The call center industry has a much shorter existence than the telephone answering service industry. While some, such as Mark Hastings, traced the beginning of the call center industry to "the divestiture of AT&T in 1984 and the subsequent explosion of 800 number usage," (DeHaan, 1998), others give the industry an earlier date of birth. Doctor Kathryn Jackson stated in 1998 that the industry was only about "twenty-five years old," (1998a, p. 198 & 1998b, p. 113). However, Tom Mikol asserted that call centers have been around "for more than thirty years," (1997, p. 70). He added that "1997 marks the thirtieth anniversary of AT&T's introduction of 800 numbers" (1997, p. 80), an essential tool of the call center industry (Perkins & Anton, 1997). Regardless of who was right, it is apparent that the call center industry's history is much shorter than that of the telephone answering service industry, which was previously identified to have begun in 1918. With the call center industry covering a shorter time span, industry participants also have a correspondingly shorter existence, ranging from "a few months to more than 30 years", but with the average life span of 8.6 years (Perkins & Anton, 1997, p. 80).

Facts about the scope and size of the call center industry are even more prevalent, with an increasing disparity of agreement. According to MCI, "in the U.S. alone, there are more than sixty thousand call centers," they further claimed that in 1995, "four out five companies operated some sort of call center," (MCI, 1997, p. 2). Jon Anton and Anne Nickerson upped this total to seventy-five thousand call centers (1998). John Goodman, of the Call Center Industry Advisory Group, increased the count even further to 100,000 (1998). However, Frost and Sullivan, a marketing consulting firm, noted that "there are more than a thousand companies [outsourcing] call center services to business customers," (Frost & Sullivan, 1999, p. 34). The enormous difference between this final figure of one thousand outsourcing call centers and the previous statistics ranging from sixty-five to one hundred thousand, suggests that the majority of call centers are in fact internal operations, handling only the call center needs of their own organization.

In contrast to the telephone answering service industry's propensity for 24 x 7 operation, a recent study by TCS Management Group reported that only forty-six percent of call centers are open twenty-four hours-a-day, seven days-a-week (Lawrence, 1998). Another striking contrast between the two industries is that, unlike the telephone answering service industry, toll-free numbers are the mainstay of the call center industry – and significant for the telephone industry as well. MCI noted that eighty percent of all toll-free traffic is answered by call centers (MCI, 1997).

In 1997, over 9.3 million people were employed in the call center industry (Thorton, 1999a). However, MCI put that mark at a much lower number of five million (MCI, 1997). This essentially matched the DMA's 1999 figure of 5.1 million (Karr, 1999c). Even lower still was the 1998 estimate of three million (Anton & Nickerson, 1998). Interestingly, this same figure was concurred with by Goodman (1998). Lower still is Klasnic (1997, p. 24) who stated there are "approximately

1,550,000 agent positions in the U.S." It is unclear what he meant by the term "positions" whether it was the number of physical "seats" or the actual number of agents employed. If he meant "seats" (which can be used twenty-four hours-a-day, seven days-a-week) the number of employees needed to fill those seats could easily track with the aforementioned three million. Contrast these figures to Read (1998), who looking only at "small" call centers (with less than seventy-five seats), claimed that this group alone accounted for a total of 990,466 seats in 1998. He also stated that "small call centers ... are the fastest growing segment in the call center market," (p. 28). In total, these call centers handle an astounding eleven billion calls annually (Anton & Nickerson, 1998).

In 1997, the value of the goods and products sold by the call center industry was $435 billion and was predicted to be $490 billion by the end of 1999 (Thorton, 1999a). Gene Gray put this figure at $460 billion for 1998 (1999, p.90) but Dresner upped it considerably to $600 billion (1998, p. 52).

As far as actual industry revenues are concerned, Dianne Porter called it a "four billion U.S. call center market," (1999a, p. 22). Whereas Frost and Sullivan (1999) stated that it is $18.3 billion industry and this being only for those call centers who handle outsourcing from other companies (that is, excluding in-house call centers). These statistics are summarized in Table 6.

Doctor Jackson, familiar with these numbers, pointed out that they were all estimates. She correctly stated that "there's no industry code" for call centers, making accurate counting impossible. Also, she added that many companies failed to consider that the department with the people answering the phones is, by definition, a call center (1998a, p.201). She placed similar suspicions on many of the other industry "facts" bandied about.

Just as in the telephone answering service industry, the call center industry is labor intensive. Morrow (1997) stated that forty-five percent of a typical call center's budget was spent on labor. Jon Anton, of Purdue University, put the level much higher, stating that in his investigation, "the human resource budget, as a percent of the total budget, averages a staggering 60% across all industries," (Anton & Nickerson, 1998, p. 86). More definitively, surveys of the call center industry by Purdue University pegged the number at sixty-eight percent in 1997 (Anton, 1997), but down to fifty-six percent in 1999 (Anton, 1999b). In both studies, this figure included four percent spent on hiring and training (Anton, 1997 & 1999c). Penny Reynolds did not advance any numbers but identified staffing costs as "the overwhelming majority of ongoing expense," (1999, p. 74).

Table 6: <u>Call Center – Vital Statistics</u>

Category	Range of Reported Values
Age of industry	15 to 30 years
Average age of industry call centers	8.6 years
Number of call centers	65,000 to 100,000
Percent of call centers operating 24 x 7	46%
Size of workforce	3 to 9.3 million
Number of seats	990,466 to 1,550,000
Annual sales	$435 to 600 billion
Annual revenues	$4 to 18.3 billion
Annual number of calls handled	11 billion

The issue of labor is compounded by staffing levels and scheduling. If call centers are overstaffed, they spend needlessly on labor, leading to inefficiencies and financial loses, while if they are understaffed, it leads to poor service, low morale, high turnover, and ultimately drives away customers (Reynolds, 1999 & Anton, 1999b).

Hourly pay rates for TSRs in the catalog call center segment of the industry were between $8.50 and $12.50 an hour (Allimadi, 1999b). The American Teleservices Association's figures put average TSRs compensation at $8.52 an hour for full-time workers and $8.00 an hour for part-time. Add to this a lengthy list of employee benefits (see Table 7), including paid vacation, holidays, and time off, health plans, 401k benefits, and bonuses (Thorton, 1999b). Purdue University's 1997 benchmarking survey, determined the hourly wage figure to be a much higher $10.76 per hour (Anton, 1997). However, according to Leo Toledo (1999), it was estimated that a full-time call center TSR costs about forty thousand dollars a year; this includes loaded payroll costs and ongoing training.

The ratio of full-time to part-time employees was also tracked. According to Milton Allimadi, full-time agents comprised forty percent of the call center workforce (up to seventy-five percent for catalog call centers), whereas five years ago, full-time staff made up only twenty-five percent (Allimadi, 1999b). The TCS Management Group study determined that "the majority of agents ... were full time," with "just under 20% of the call centers [having] no part-time agents at all," (Lawrence, 1998, p. 58). Perkin's and Anton's findings concur with Allimadi. In Purdue University's 1997 survey, forty-four percent of the respondents "indicated they had no part-time employees" (Perkins & Anton, 1997, p.82).

Table 7: <u>ATA List of Call Center Employee Benefits (and Compensation)</u>

Benefit	Percent of Firms Providing
Paid vacation, holidays, and time-off	96%
Health plans for employees and families	85%
401k plans for employees	75%
Tuition reimbursement	49%
Individual bonuses	43%
Profit sharing plans	25%
Team bonuses	24%
Perfect attendance awards	23%
Medical reimbursement plans	21%
Matching contributions for charitable giving	15%
Hourly compensation rate (ATA)	$8.00 to $8.52
(Hourly compensation rate – other sources	$8.50 to $12.50)

Hiring Call Center Agents

Ten to fifteen percent of the human resource budget is strictly for the recruitment, hiring, and training of new TSRs (Anton & Nickerson, 1998); this equates to being six to nine percent of the total budget. The Purdue University benchmarking surveys put it lower at four percent of the total budget (Anton, 1997 & 1999). Regardless of the actual number, lowering employee attrition rates will have the impact of correspondingly reducing hiring and training costs.

Anton and Nickerson advocated a seven-step system for the successful hiring of new TSRs. First, was to use voice mail to "profile" the candidates, screening out those who did not meet certain basic criteria. Next, a "telephone voice assessment" should be conducted to ensure they have sufficient telephone communications qualities and attributes. Those who successfully passed these first two screens would be given an aptitude test. The fourth step was to conduct a "job preview" covering basic characteristics and expectations of the job. If the candidates were still interested at that point, the candidate should sit with an experienced TSR to witness firsthand the type and scope of the work. For candidates who passed these screens and remained interested in the position, it would be appropriate to conduct a live interview. For high-level TSR positions, a "role play" session would appropriately follow if the candidate was successful in the interview. Lastly, a background check should be conducted of all successful candidates before they are offered a position (Anton & Nickerson, 1998, pp. 90-96).

Jackson (1998a) acknowledged that just to hire a TSR (not including training) costs twelve hundred dollars. Part of this high cost was that call centers typically interview seven applicants for each new hire (Anton, 1999a). In 1998, the total cost to hire and fully train a new agent to be online and successfully handling calls was an average of $5,000. This included both the costs to recruit, screen, test, and hire, as well as the cost of the subsequent training required to permit them to fully and successfully process calls on their own (Anton & Nickerson, 1998). For 1999, this figure jumped to an astonishing $6,398 (Anton, 1999b). Unfortunately, Lenz stated that a majority of new hires were not retained by the call center after training is completed (1999, p. 6). Lucia Rocca summed it up succinctly, "It costs too much to lose people," (Thorton, 1999b).

The length of time spent on training was also a consideration. "Four weeks should be the standard," because shorter times leads to both retention and quality problems (Lenz, 1999, p. 6). The TCS Management Group pinpointed the actual number of hours training to average 131 (which is roughly three weeks and two days); they also added that ongoing training was an average of seventy-three hours per year (Porter, 1999b). Purdue University placed the average number of training hours somewhat higher, at 186 (Anton, 1997); this roughly equates to four weeks and three days. These 186 hours of training time were divided between classroom instruction (forty-eight percent) and on-the-job training (fifty-two) percent (Anton, 1997). Jackson foresaw a call center training simulator in the near future (1998a); this would allow training times to be reduced and TSR efficacy to improve.

Employee Retention

Turnover is another concern in the call center industry. Anton and Nickerson stated that the turnover rate is "in excess of 100%" at some call centers (1998, p. 86). They added that "the single biggest challenge for call center managers today is finding enough talented people to handle the pressure of a constant stream of ... calls," (p. 86). To complicate matters, "many of the good people hired to be TSRs do not really fit this line of work and quit," (p. 88). This is further compounded by a tight job market and record low unemployment (Lenz, 1999). While the 1997 Purdue University study put TSR turnover (for inbound call centers) at a relatively low seventeen percent (Anton, 1997), the 1999 study showed that it jumped to twenty-six percent turnover for full-time TSRs and thirty-four percent for part-time TSRs (Anton, 1999b). See Table 8.

Table 8: <u>Call Center – Human Resource Statistics</u>

Category	Range of Reported Values
Direct labor costs (percentage of budget)	45 to 68%
Hiring & training costs (percentage of budget)	4 to 9%
TSR hourly rate (full time)	$8.52 to $12.50
TSR hourly rate (part time)	$8.00
Percent of full time TSRs	40 to 75%
Average cost to hire and train a TSR	$ 6,398
Time to train a TSR	131 to 186 hours
Time spent on classroom training (percent)	52%
Time spent with hands-on training (percent)	48%
TSR turnover rate (full-time)	26%
TSR turnover rate (part-time)	34%

Mary Lenz provided several useful and relevant points in her 1999 article, "Grappling with Agent Turnover." First, she stated that TSRs want to feel "like they are part of the team" and that they need a "mission and be given the reasons to believe in it." She faulted training for this lapse, as there is little said about the important functions and critical purposes of TSRs during the training process. Once the TSR has completed their initial training, ongoing training can "address issues like coping with stress and burnout," helping to minimize turnover and increase retention. Also, there is not enough done to chart and plan career paths and advancement opportunities for TSRs. She challenged the industry to help TSRs think of their jobs as professions. She showed that where this has been accomplished, TSRs "often stay for years," greatly reducing employee churn (Lenz, 1999, p. 6).

Scott Thorton (1999b) concurred, that "a definite career path can help immediately in reducing turn-over," (p. 66) and he added, "employee benefits are one of the key ways to demonstrate professional and personal regard for employees," (p. 67). Call Center Management's internet publication, *QueueTips* also addressed TSR turnover. In it, Brad Cleveland detailed twelve reasons for TSR turnover and low morale (Appendix F) and offered four prescriptions to proactively address employee losses and combat it in a positive manner. His first recommendation was to "broaden and extend the training [that] agents receive and the responsibilities they have." Next, involve them in various aspects of "managing the call center," allowing them added responsibility and a chance to develop a sense of ownership. Thirdly, ensure that they understand and buy into the "direction and values of the organization." Lastly, make sure that the call center is providing good service levels to callers, thereby reducing TSR anxiety and frustrations in the first place (QueueTips, 1999a, p. 2).

Greg Levin also advocated the development of TSR career paths and advised call center managers to "develop different 'micro' job tiers for which the agent can strive," assigning new titles to reflect these positions, but warning that in doing so they must have substance and not be merely titles. "Empowering agents and creating job diversity," he stated, "is essential to retaining staff in a small call center for as long as possible," (QueueTips, 1999a, p. 3).

Most critical among factors leading to the high turnover of TSRs are low compensation levels, with inadequate pay given as a major cause. When TSRs leave as a result of being under-compensated, costs to the call center increase as a result of the ensuing efforts to hire and train replacements, the need for increased management supervision, and the resulting reduction in productivity. Call centers must begin to track the full cost of turnover in order to justify an increase in wages to correct the problem. Many call centers pay slightly more than fast food restaurants and end up getting a slightly better employee. A higher paid TSR is generally more reliable and more productive. In addition to better pay, also mentioned were aggressive retention programs to keep TSRs on the payroll and from leaving with valuable training and knowledge, sometimes taking it to a competitor. Quite simply, call centers can no longer afford to "undervalue their most important asset," (Reiners, 1999, p. 36).

Anton and Nickerson listed five core competencies that TSRs should possess in order to be a right match for the position and to be successful working in a call center. They are to be able to: 1) simultaneously think, talk, and type, 2) listen with empathy, 3) be attentive to details, 4) express ideas clearly, and 5) solve problems (1998). Proactive efforts to seek candidates with these characteristics will likewise serve to reduce employee churn.

The proper management of the TSRs is also a critical factor; not only to combat high turnover but also for performance issues. In most call centers, TSRs are directly managed by supervisors. It is imperative for there to be an appropriate ratio of TSRs to supervisors. Fourteen agents to one supervisor (1999a) is the number advanced by Doctor Anton. Porter essentially agrees with this figure but gave a wider range of eleven to twenty TSRs per supervisor depending on the circumstances and the type of call center (1999b).

Over ninety-five percent of supervisors are assigned the responsibilities of doing coaching and quality monitoring (Lawrence, 1998). Quality monitoring can be used to improve the efficacy of TSRs by not only catching errors, but also through positive reinforcement. The results are not only better, more effective employees, but also a reduction in turnover (Elwell, 1999). Eighty-three percent of the call centers surveyed used "traditional silent monitoring" for their quality programs and over half recorded some calls for later evaluation; about twenty percent record all calls (Lawrence, 1998). Monitoring was deemed so relevant that *TeleProfessional* magazine's 1998 industry audit included monitoring as one of their five major ranking criteria (Karr, 1998). Coaching, unlike monitoring, is done sitting next to the TSR and not done remotely or at a later time. The purpose of coaching is to provide immediate feedback about TSR performance, coaching them to improve. All these ideas about dealing with turnover are covered in Figure 1.

Anton (1999b) stated that the five most common TSR performance measurements in the call center industry are: 1) call quality monitoring, 2) attendance, 3) call handle time, 4) caller satisfaction results, and 5) input accuracy. Of these, attendance and input accuracy are self-explanatory; quality monitoring has already been covered. Call handle time will be covered later in the section on call center metrics. The remaining item is caller satisfaction results. Research by the TCS Management Group showed that over half of the call centers polled used some form of caller satisfaction assessment mechanism; many call centers used multiple methods (Lawrence, 1998).

Purdue University put the number of call centers, with a formal mechanism to gather call feedback, slightly higher at sixty-one percent (Anton, 1999b). The most common technique was a mail-in survey, with telephone surveys coming in second. Larger call centers tended to outsource the telephone surveys to other call centers, whereas small call centers had staff conduct their own appraisals (Lawrence, 1998).

- Help TSRs feel part of the team.

- Communicate corporate mission.

- Provide training on dealing with stress and burnout.

- Chart career path.

- Provide ongoing training.

- Delegate more responsibility.

- Staff appropriately for expected traffic

- Improve compensation and benefits.

- Hire for key competencies:

- Simultaneously talk, type, think.

- Listen with empathy.

- Be attentive to details.

- Express ideas clearly.

- Solve problems.

- Proper supervision and management:

- Monitoring.

- Coaching.

- Maintain proper supervisor to TSR ratios.

Figure 1. Recommended Ideas to Reduce Turnover.

Call Center Metrics

Most call centers use some method of tracking and comparing their statistical results with other call centers, industry norms, or accepted standards. Increasingly, benchmarking is a tool used by leading call centers as an effective way to determine what their statistical goals should be. "Benchmarking is conducted to find best practices," stated Doctor Jackson. Surveys "simply tell you what other call centers are doing," she added, which "may not be a best practice," (1998a, p. 198). "Best practices benchmarking," stated Richard Lawrence, "is intended to help organizations match their operational policies and practices to those of specific call centers they have identified as best in class," (1998, p. 54). While one would assume an inverse correlation between call volume and statistical achievement, Sharna Kahn sites a case study in which quantitative performance metrics improved during times of peak call center traffic (1999).

The aforementioned Doctor Jon Anton, from Purdue University, has been conducting call center industry benchmarking for several years. The metrics of the 1999 call center survey painted a contrasting picture to the 1998 ATSI telephone answering service survey. The call center metrics are displayed in Table 9, while a comparison of analogous answering service and call center metrics are summarized in Table 10. The study revealed that it took an average of thirty-six seconds to answer calls. These calls lasted over four minutes and took more than three minutes of follow-up work after the caller hung up. Over ninety-four percent of the calls were answered, meaning that roughly five percent hung up before they could be answered; callers did, however, wait an average of seventy seconds before disconnecting. TSRs at these call centers were busy attending to the needs of their callers approximately seventy-five percent of the time (Anton, 1999b).

The comparison of statistics between the telephone answering and call center industries is noteworthy, as well as illustrative. The significant differences are much longer call durations and higher occupancy rates for call centers, but greater responsiveness on the part of the telephone answering services.

System utilization is "the planned hours of use versus the actual login hours" (p. 56), with realistic numbers ranging from seventy-eight to eighty-three percent; this is a result of TSR breaks, procedures to log in and out, and time spent on coaching or ongoing training (Mandaro, 1999).

Table 9: <u>Call Center Service Level Metrics (1998)</u>

Category	Median
Speed of answer	36.0 seconds
Talk time	4.3 minutes
Wrap-up time	3.2 minutes
(Total call time	7.5 minutes)
Calls abandoned	5.4%
Time in queue	49.7 seconds
Time before abandoning	69.5 seconds
Occupancy Rate	76 to 83%
Utilization Rate	65 to 70%

Table 10: Comparison of Service Level Metrics (1998)

Category	Answering Service	Call Center	Unit
Wait time/speed to answer	14	36	seconds
Hold time/queue time	29	50	seconds
Time per call	49	450	seconds
Occupancy Rate	47	76	percent

Occupancy, on the other hand, is the amount of time a TSR is actually working compared to the amount of time scheduled. This is comprised of "talk time" which is time on-line talking with callers, and "wrap-up time" or the amount of work done after the call is completed. Talk time ranges from sixty-five to seventy percent, while wrap-up time is in the five to ten percent range (Mandaro, 1999). Added together these figures result in an occupancy rate of seventy to eighty percent. Anton's 1997 survey agreed with this range pegging agent occupancy at an arithmetic mean of seventy-seven percent, with an average actual goal of eight-one percent (1997, p. 7).

Responsiveness to callers can be measured in several ways. One method is the "abandonment rate." When a caller is on hold waiting to talk with a TSR and they elect to hang-up, rather than continue to wait, it is an called an "abandoned" call. By comparing the number of abandoned calls to "presented" calls (that is, calls which are presented to the system – they will either abandon or be answered), the percentage of calls abandoned can be determined and tracked.

Although it is not feasible to totally eliminate the number of callers which abandon, call centers do make an effort to minimize it. Purdue University's 1999 benchmarking survey placed the average abandonment rate at 5.4% and the median rate at 4.3% (Anton, 1999b, p. 5-7). This is a decrease from their 1997 survey results of an average abandonment rate of six percent (Anton, 1997, p. 6). Interestingly, Prognostics, a company which conducts customer satisfaction research, quantified the perceptions of callers who were placed on hold. They determined that callers on hold for one minute perceived they were actually on hold for one minute. However, when left on hold for two minutes their perception was that it was three minutes. Three minutes of hold time resulted in a perception of five; four minutes seemed like nine, five became fifteen, and ten minutes felt like thirty (Rose, 1998, p. 116). Jackson cited research which verified that callers who abandon do, in fact, call back later (1998a). However, she did not provide the ratio of those who do to those who do not. Regardless, abandoned calls do result in lost business. Interestingly, both the 1997 and 1999 Purdue studies reported that some call centers had a zero percent abandonment rate (Anton, 1997, p. 6 and 1999, p. 5-7). While it is possible for this to occur during relatively short periods of time, the only way to assure it can be maintained long-term is to have as many lines and agents as there are potential callers, which is an absurdity. However, if the number of lines is limited to the number of agents, then every call will be answered immediately and will not have the opportunity to abandon. The side-effect of this is that many callers will receive a busy signal, therefore they will not even get an opportunity to hang-up while they are on hold. Therefore, the number of "busies" or "calls blocked" is another way of measuring call center responsiveness. The preceding Purdue research documented blocked calls to be an average of five percent in 1997 (Anton, 1997, p. 6) and 7.97 percent in 1999; the median figure for 1999 was 4.84 percent (Anton, 1999b, p. 5-7). Marissa Morrow claims that callers who do get a busy signal have a probability of calling back seventy to eighty percent of the time (1997). This implies that the twenty to thirty percent who get a busy signal never call back. Regardless, if callers call back or not, blocked calls are another representation of caller responsiveness.

Outsourcing

It was previously inferred, in the section on call center statistics, that the vast majority of call centers were actually internal operations and that only a small minority provided outsourcing services (that is, provided call center services to other companies).

A 1995 study revealed that eleven percent of call centers in the United States outsourced work to other call centers; that figure was projected to double to twenty-two percent by 2000 (Tehrani, 1997). While this prediction may prove to be too optimistic, the 1999 Purdue benchmarking study did demonstrate an increase in call center outsourcing activity, with 12.8 percent of the respondents outsourcing some of their calls. It was noted that for this group the principal reason was to outsource overflow calls to other firms (Anton, 1999b, p. 1-2).

Lori Fentem concurred that this is an emergent development and noted that most call center activity is for the primary purpose of new customer acquisition. Increasingly, large call centers understand and appreciate that outsourcing call center efforts allows them to better focus on their core competencies. This permits their outsourcing call center partners to provide them with the requisite call processing expertise. The result of this is that it serves to minimize risk and maximize their return on investment, both of which are good business strategies. (Fentem, 1997).

Dorothy Young took a more aggressive stance, stating that "the benefits of outsourcing and its impact on financial performance are now hard facts," (Young, 1998, p. 64). She cited the "growing popularity of outsourcing" as evidence to support this, arguing that companies have resorted to outsourcing because they realize they cannot execute all ancillary activities which their enterprise requires with adequate ease and success. As such, they elect to outsource these tasks in order to focus on their core competencies and channel limited financial and human resources to those areas which will provide the best return and the biggest value (Young, 1998).

It was noted by Peter Theis that call centers who provide services to other companies typically utilize a shared group of resources (that is, staff, equipment, telephone lines, etc.) to be shared as needed by all of their client companies. In doing so, they achieve economies-of-scale and are able to provide services at a cost advantage which their clients could not realize. He calls this approach an "unrestricted allocation" of facilities. The concern is that one client, with a burst of calls, would capture and dominate all available resources, in effect blocking out all of the other clients' callers. To address this, Theis advocated implementing "dynamic allocation" in which each client enjoys a limited number of lines (and presumably staff) dedicated to their project, with other lines (and presumably staff) being dynamically appropriated as call traffic warrants. He advanced that unrestricted allocation tends to benefit the larger client companies, whereas dynamic allocation skews in favor of the midsize and smaller organizations (Theis, 1999b, p. 59).

Call Center Technology

It is apparent, from the vast quantity of writing on the subject, that staffing issues are the primary concern when dealing with call center matters. Although technology receives less attention, especially from the general media, it is no less a critical part of the call center equation. In fact, without the technology behind the call center, it would not be feasible to process calls. Diane Porter summed it up by saying that "if something goes wrong with the technology, chances are good that production will grind to a screeching halt," (Porter, 1999b, p. 49). For this critical reason, technology was one of the five areas of focus in *TeleProfessional* magazine's audit of call centers. Specifically, they addressed five technologies which they determined as being key differentiating traits. These included computer-telephone integration (CTI), interactive voice response (IVR), call routing, predictive dialing, and call blending. Call centers needed to have at least three of these technologies implemented in order to receive a "high" ranking (Karr, 1998b). Of these five, predictive dialing is strictly an outbound call center technology. Whereas call blending only applies to centers which perform both inbound and outbound (they "blend," or co-mingle both the types of calling). Conversely call routing, or automatic call distribution (ACD), is appropriately an inbound call center technology, which allows calls to be effectively routed to the proper person or department or the most available agent.

CTI allows the telephone system and computer network to be amalgamated, functioning as a seamless unit and permitting the computer screen to track the phone call. Derek Slater labeled both ACD and CTI as being "reasonable mature technologies" and common among most call centers (1999).

ACD and other call routing techniques are nearly universal in call centers. While ACD is the more traditional call routing tool, sending each caller "to the next available agent," advanced call routing goes way beyond that basic level. Skills-based routing is one such popular result, which allows calls to be routed to the agent most skilled in handling a certain type of call. This focus on skills-based routing has, however, added many levels of complexity to the singular goal of getting calls answered quickly. While this detracts from some of the efficiency gains of the traditional ACD (Anderson & Taylor, 1998) or destroys it (Karr, 1999a), it is nonetheless implemented by forty-two percent of the call centers surveyed. Language routing was critical (Slater, 1999) and frequently cited use of skills-based routing equipment (Lawrence, 1998).

After ACD systems, IVR is the next most commonly used call center technology (Lawrence, 1998). The next generation of voice processing equipment will employ speech-recognition algorithms, which after years of languishing in the labs, is now showing immense promise (Karr, 1999a).

Another call center innovation is workforce management systems, which are in use in about half of all call centers (Lawrence, 1998).

When considering all of the equipment and technical expertise present in most call centers, Brad Cleveland was prompted to declare that an investment in call center technology was a principal tactical component for any industry or business (Bianchi, 1999). A list of these key technologies is shown in Figure 2.

- CTI – Computer-Telephony Integration

- IVR – Interactive Voice Response

- ACD – Automatic Call Distribution

- Skills-based routing

- Workforce management systems

Figure 2. Key Call Center Technologies.

Virtual Call Centers

A virtual call center may be an oxymoron since it cannot be a center and also be virtual. Nevertheless, the concept of a virtual or distributed call center is one that has garnered some recent attention. David Kopf noted that there is a trend among call centers to move towards being decentralized. One reason to do so might have been the result of a merger, in which it was necessary to maintain two disparate centers. However, more common reasons included disaster recovery (if one site has facility problems, the other site can take over), tapping new labor markets, or to merely link two centers together for overflow purposes. If the decision to go virtual is because one wishes to connect two separate sites together, then a greater economy of scale will result. In the past, the primary roadblock to setting up a virtual call center was the technology required to allow the far-flung locations to function effectively as one unit. Now, that difficulty has been simplified by various technological advances and innovations. The real difficulty comes after the technology has been put into place and the virtual center implemented. That problem is determining how to effectively manage the new entity. When a call center becomes distributed, centralized management control is no longer an option; supervision too must also be decentralized. This results in increased management expenses and a reversal in overhead economy-of-scale. To be cost-effective, any decision to decentralize must hold the promise of sufficient benefits in order to overcome these increased overhead costs (Kopf, 1999). As such, the geographical dispersal of a call center has its complexity increased and renders successful operations more difficult to define and to measure (Mandaro & Wilson, 1999). These are shown in Figure 3.

Pros

- Disaster recovery

- Handle overflow calls

- Tap into new labor market

- Increase economy of scale

Cons

- Increased technology/equipment requirements

- Harder to manage

- Decentralized supervision

- Increased overhead

Figure 3. Pros and Cons of Virtual Call Centers.

Many call centers are aware of these limitations and the intricacies of running a dispersed call center. As a consequence, it is not surprising that fifty-two percent of all call centers have, therefore, one centralized location. Thirty-six percent, in fact, have two to five locations and only eleven percent have six or more locations (Perkins & Anton, 1997).

The ultimate extreme of a virtual call center is to extend its effective boundary and reach into employees' homes, allowing for telecommuting, or working at home. Although, this thought is a compelling and enticing concept, very few call centers have actually pursued and implemented it. In fact, over ninety-one percent of call centers admitted to have no TSRs working at home (Perkins & Anton, 1997). Their hesitation stemmed not so much from the technical aspects, but again from the management issues revolving around supervising a geographically dispersed and isolated workforce (Karr, 1999a). Thirty-nine percent of all companies indicated that while they felt their business could effectively make use of some degree of telecommuting, only nineteen percent were willing to even advance it as an option for their employees. The obvious benefits of telecommuting are reduced facility expenses at the corporate office and the opportunity to reach into a new and untapped labor market. Much of management's fear, relating to the supervision of home-based TSRs, can be alleviated by selecting the right individuals to participate. Although telecommuting is off to a slow start, the Gartner Group predicted that twenty-five to forty percent of all call center agents will be telecommuting, at least part of the time, by 2002 (Karr, 1999b).

Terry Ghio explained that the virtual call center employs network-based routing to extend the physical walls of the call center into the real world. Anywhere there is a connection to the internet or the switched telephone network, there is the opportunity for an agent station to be connected to a virtual call center and for a location-independent TSR to log in and process calls. Ghio reiterated some of the previous benefits of a distributed call center, as well as mentioning some additional reasons. Two of them, expanding the labor pool and reducing facility costs, have already been pointed out. Additionally, virtual call centers allow for piecework compensation, offer improved morale and better motivation, and provide the ability to tap into agents with specialized skill sets when needed (Ghio, 1999). "With the emergence of IP (internet protocol) telephony," stated David Reiners, we can expect "a wave of non-traditional, distributed call centers." These can be connected anywhere the organization's network reaches, including the internet (Reiners, 1999, p. 39).

With such a list of benefits and the technological opportunities behind them, especially the internet, it should come as no surprise that telecommuting is growing and will continue to do so in the future. The Gartner Group measured this growth to be approximately twenty percent a year (Allimadi, 1999a).

Contact Centers

Carter Lusher, of the Gartner Group, asserted that call centers are becoming "more like contact centers," able to serve customers regardless of how they elect to contact the call center, whether it be by a telephone call, letter, fax, email, web site, or even "interactive video kiosk" (Bianchi, 1998, p. 38). Although the term contact center is conceptuality accurate, the call center label will stick for the time being, covering a wide array of different transactions, including "reservation centers, help desks, information lines, customer service centers, even 911 numbers" (Bianchi, 1998, p. 40). Bill Burr concurred when he stated that, "call centers will morph into customer contact centers." He conceded that traditional voice telephone calls will continue to comprise the majority of contacts for the near future, but that increasingly customers will seek other modes of contact, chiefly via the internet (Durr, 1999, p. 40). Lou Volpe advanced the concept further, stating that the traditional call center will turn into a "dynamic customer contact center," serving as "a kind of customer intelligence center, breaking down barriers between customer and company," (Volpe, 1999, p. 92). A list of these new labels for call centers is found in Figure 4.

Scott Thorton, however, maintained that the term "contact center" has already replaced the moniker of call center in some circles. This, he argued, is merely a reflection of the multitude of ways in which our society is beginning to conduct business. The call center industry has "a remarkable capacity to adapt" to technology changes and economic shifts, "yet the greatest changes are in front of us, not behind us," (Thorton, 1999b, p. 67). In fact, Thorton quoted an unnamed source as having estimated that seventy percent of all inbound call centers have already made this leap into becoming a contact center, or at least plan to do so within one year. He also substituted the term "universal call center" for his previously declared label of "contact center" (Thorton, 1999a, p. 9).

- Contact center

- Multimedia call center

- Web-enabled call center

- Universal call center

- Telechannel

Figure 4. Names for the Next Generation Call Center.

In his article, "The New Combat Zone," Doctor Bill Bleuel agreed with the contact center concept, but avoided naming it for fear that a new label would be out-of-date by the time his article was published. Bleuel envisaged today's call center as a "conglomeration of technologies designed to accommodate the ever-changing world," (1999, p. 9). Call centers are adding fax and email as contact methods and even implementing web-site buttons to connect a customer to the contact center, over the internet. Bleuel advised call center managers to begin now to aggressively move in this new direction, implementing the technological infrastructure to make it all work.

By amassing multiple connection methods to the call center, such as fax, email, and web-based contact, more components of customer communication are introduced, and an additional layer of complexity is added to today's call center in order to form a contact center (Mandaro & Wilson, 1999). Victor Wortman used the term "multimedia" to describe the vast array of connection options existing in the evolving contact center. It is evolving so fast that there are no real experts to guide and direct this effort. The challenge, then, is to integrate all of the organization's databases into the evolving array of connection options. This removes the call centers' status as merely organizational overhead and positions it strategically in the focal point of corporate activity (Wortman, 1999).

While Wortman used the term "multimedia," to describe this compilation of contact methodology, Sara Frankl reported on the development of the "telechannel," citing an Oxford Associates' survey covering one fourth of the Fortune 1000 companies. Their work uncovered that the leaders of these companies are investing heavily in the telechannel to establish and enhance their competitive advantage.

They envision this effort will pay huge dividends by "driving revenue growth, improving customer loyalty and retention and lowering sales and customer service costs," (Frankl, 1999, p. 17). Their work identified crucial pressures driving this effort, including a growing customer demand for twenty-four-hour support and the acknowledgement of the telephone as an increasingly critical and ubiquitous business tool; furthermore, the growing success of the internet will do nothing but exacerbate these dynamics (Frankl, 1999). It is good that these companies are taking such aggressive steps, because a study by Matrixx Marketing revealed that only seventeen percent of Fortune 500 companies answer their email. (Liebeskind, 1998). *Call Center Management Review* confirmed this sad fact. They reported that most companies failed to respond at all to email messages or if they do, it takes several weeks. Often these tardy communications included incorrect information, were sentence fragments framed in incomplete thoughts, and contained spelling and grammatical errors (QueueTips, 1999b). In a similar vein, Jupiter Communications reported that in their research of 125 web sites, only fifty-eight percent responded to email within five days (Read, 1999a). In his article, "Dawning of a New Era," Brad Cleveland said that while the performance objective for a telephone call is service level, the "performance objective" for an email is "response time," (Cleveland, 1999, p. 114). While agreeing that response time is the number one concern, Bill Rose took it a step further adding that the "second issue is resolve time." In other words, a quick response is worthless if it contains the wrong information (Rose, 1998, p. 116). Matrixx Marketing, which provides outsourced email response service, boasts a far better response record than the preceding statistics, stating that they answer all their email within eighteen hours (Liebeskind, 1998).

DirecTV reported that they received about 300,000 telephone calls a month, but only six hundred email messages, which is about two-tenths of one percent. Andrea Jacobs indicated, however, that this number is on the increase due to the company's internet presence. They do expect that email communications with subscribers to become a vital process in the future. This simple fact, that businesses are using email, is further proof that call centers must become contact centers, allowing customer interaction to occur using any available media (Liebeskind, 1998).

This was best demonstrated by the catalog call centers. This subset of the call center industry is vigorously searching for methods to migrate their customer communications away from the telephone and on to other contact center technologies. Toward this end, the *State of the Catalog Industry* study showed that in 1998 almost seventy-five percent of the catalog companies already had an internet presence. Several catalog companies took this effort very seriously, planning to shift up to one fourth of their sales and support activities to their web site. Even so, it was noted that "customers still primarily...trust...companies that offer live service over the phone" (Allimadi, 1999b, p.68). Figure 5 lists the types of services which can be offered by a contact center.

- Phone Calls

- Faxes

- Email

- Text chat (web chat, live text chat, click-to-chat)

- Call back buttons

- Talk buttons (VoIP, Cybercall, click-to-talk)

Figure 5. Contact Center Services.

The Internet

It is apparent from the numerous articles on contact centers that the internet has played, and will continue to play, a key role in the migration from call center to contact center. In recognition of this trend, the 1999 Purdue University benchmark study asked participants which internet features they used on their web sites. A slight majority, at 51.7%, included a toll-free number for web surfers to call should they need additional assistance. Slightly less than half (49.3%) said they had email addresses or email links for the purpose of facilitating communication with web-site visitors. Twenty-eight percent of the companies had configured their sites to allow customers the ability for "self-service," that is to provide the means for them to answer their own questions (Anton, 1999b, p. 5-16). It is worthy to note that, according to the Forrester Group, self-service via the internet versus traditional support using toll-free numbers has been shown to reduce costs by forty-three percent (Read, 1999a). A small minority used "cybercall" (1.7%) and "call back buttons" (1.5%) (Anton, 1999b, p. 5-16). This type of "live service from a web site is still new," stated Joe Fleischer, "but it won't be a novelty for long,' 1998b, p. 98).

Cybercall is a term coined to describe the provision for a voice conduit to be made from customer to contact center over the same internet connection which is being used to view the web site itself. Although this requires specialized equipment and software for both customer and company, it does allow for the dual aspects of interaction to take place simultaneously on a single phone line.

With similar intent and results, callback buttons are less complicated to implement and easier to use, although two phone lines are required for the customer. In this case, web surfers click on a web site button to indicate that they wish for a representative of the company to call them. They enter in their telephone number. Then the request and phone number are sent over the internet to the contact center; the call center automatically initiates a call to the customer who can then talk with the TSR while viewing the company's web site (Hickox, 1998). Although the amount of time it takes for this connection to be established can vary greatly, one company reported an average time of thirty-three seconds (Fleischer, 1998b); to put this time in perspective, it is roughly equivalent to listening to a phone ring five times.

It is surprising that these penetration levels for toll-free and email web services are not higher than their reported levels of fifty percent. After all, it is a trivial matter to place a toll-free number or email address on a web site, yet about half of the web sites fail to include these basic amenities. This fact did not surprise AT&T's Gary Hickox who acknowledges that in a majority of organizations the web site and call center are two disparate and independent customer contact options (Hickox, 1998). Angela Karr concurred, "Web sites represent a huge, yet untapped market for call centers willing to integrate multimedia technologies," (Karr, 1998a, p. 10). Dorothy Young was able to confirm this statistically, stating that about a third of web site inquiries go directly to call centers. Even for call center web sites this figure is only fifty percent. Through the linking of web sites to call centers, companies enjoy the potential to react faster and close sales more effectively; this translates to opportunities to increase profits (Young, 1998).

Russ Kahan referred to this integration of web site into call center as "webifying" or more commonly referred to as becoming "web-enabled" (1998, p. 116). Approximately fifteen percent of all call centers claim to already be web-enabled and this number is expected to double in one year. It was projected that by 2002 the web-enabled philosophy will have manifested itself in twenty-five percent of all call centers (Karr, 1998a). Kahan advanced three "webifying" options: "Click-to-talk," "click-to-chat," and "click-to-call-me-back," (p. 116). Click-to-talk is the same as the aforementioned cybercall, whereas click-to-call-me-back is more commonly known as the preceding call back button. Surprisingly, click-to-chat was not included in the Purdue study. Click-to-chat, also known as live text chat, allows customers and contact center agents to type messages back and forth, in real-time, using the internet as the connection medium (Fleischer, 1999a).

The term cybercall is included in the generic and more universal technology better known as voice over internet protocol (VoIP). In basic terms VoIP uses the internet to transmit voice signals. Web surfers can use this technology when viewing a properly configured web site. They click on the appropriate button and voice path is established over the internet, between them and the call center. The web surfer talks into the computer microphone and hears the call center agent over the PC's speakers or headset. In this manner, they carry on a conversation while viewing the web site (QueueTips, 1999d). Generally, the agent can see the same web page as the "caller." Sometimes there is the option for the agent to "push" web pages to the caller. According to Dresner, this "web-to-phone interface gives both the company and the web surfer what they really want – an interactive experience," (1998, p. 52). Currently, this application is viewed as a technology loser, but in reality, it is just ahead of its time. Kenneth McKenna predicted that VoIP "will grow tremendously in the future," but adds that the voice quality is not yet at the level it needs to be to be embraced on a larger scale (Karr, 1999a, p. 47). The one advantage of VoIP is that lets agents do what they were trained to do, talk to people. Even so, Joe Fleisher indicated that for the time being, most surfers prefer text chat instead. In fact, sites with VoIP generally also have text chat as a fallback technology in the event that VoIP does not work or suffers from voice quality deficiencies (Fleisher, 1999).

The reasons to web-enable one's call center are simple and straightforward. First, Scott Thorton stated that e-commerce is the "next revolution in marketing" and will make the telemarketing boom of the eighties and nineties look "mild by comparison," (Thorton, 1999a, p.9) *Call Center Solutions'* publisher Nadji Tehrani declared that e-commerce is the fastest growing of any business sector because it is "fast, convenient, and cost-effective," (Tehrani, 1998).

Angela Karr noted three significant trends to encourage the implementation of web-enabling technologies: the ongoing increase in the number of internet users, consumers becoming accustomed to the immediacy of web transactions, and email as the most popular method of electronic communication, boasting over one trillion messages a year (1998a). Kahan summed it up succinctly, stating that web-enabled call centers allow companies to "make more money" and to "give customers instant gratification," (1998, p. 10). More profound was Hickox's pronouncement that web-enabled call centers provide "the missing link between electronic and human commerce," (1998, p. 48). Only a scant few years ago, web sites were considered novelties, but have since been thrust into the limelight as a requisite business tool and marketing mechanism. As such, the web-enabled call center, or contact center, becomes more of a necessity and is recognized for its "potential to appeal to a wider range of customers than traditional call centers," (Fleischer, 1999a, p. 81). Perhaps most compelling was Jess Reed's experience that web sales double when customers can talk with a TSR (Hickox, 1998). As the price of the item for sale increases, so does a customer's reluctance to buy it over the internet. A web-enabled call center agent, however, can provide human interaction that is vital to gaining or maintaining a customer, a characteristic that a solitary web site lacks (Hickox, 1998). Fleischer suggested that even greater value is obtained by allowing web surfers to contact the company by any method they prefer, be it web chat, cybercall, call back buttons, or email (1999a) as well as the more traditional telephone call, fax, or letter.

As call centers become web-enabled, Joe Fleischer pointed out two fundamental transformations that will revolutionize the organization. First, by nature of the global ubiquity of the internet, an organization with a web-enabled call center therefore becomes an international player, boasting a global presence. Secondly, less obvious but more profound, the web site ceases to be "an electronic document" and becomes "a service" instead (Fleischer, 1998b, pp. 97-98).

With over a trillion email messages being carried on the internet annually (Karr 1998a) it is no wonder that more of them are making their way to call centers (Fleischer, 1999b). Once a web site has been accessed, email is the most frequently used method of contacting the company (Fleischer, 1998b). With this influx of traffic, technology must be implemented to ensure its quick and timely processing. It was not too long ago that email messages could be delayed for days without fear of losing a sale or alienating a customer, but that luxury of delay no longer exists (Fleischer, 1998b). Brendan Read reported that in the past customers who would be willing to wait weeks for a response to an email now expect or need a reply within hours (1999b).

With this influx of email traffic and ever-increasing response expectations, technology must be implemented to ensure its quick and timely processing. Email routing software packages are available to facilitate the organization of and rapid responding to email traffic, as well as automatically answering common questions which warrant standard responses (Fleischer, 1999b). Software to put email in queues, just as is done with live calls, also streamlines and speeds email processing (Sweat, 1999).

The costs of email are also an issue. In the article, "The Modern Call Center," several numbers were advanced as the cost to process an email, from a low of fifty cents to a high of eighteen dollars. Regardless, it is less than the cost to respond to a letter, priced at about twenty-five dollars. Purdue's Anton pegged a phone call at three dollars, but Network Associates put it much higher at $7.50 (Riggs & Thyfault, 1999). However, Bill Rose placed the cost of a phone call even higher, starting at around nine dollars (Rose, 1998). A web chat session was stated to cost about one dollar (assuming that the agent has three or four simultaneous sessions in progress). It was noted that the drafting of email responses is one that should be done warily and only wisely selected and screened individuals should be allowed to perform this critical task. Many agents can carry on an excellent conversation over the phone but are unable to effectively communicate a coherent or cogent thought in written form (Riggs & Thyfault, 1999). It should be noted that Matrixx Marketing, which provides email processing to its outsourcing clients, charges fifty cents to respond to an email. This, along with fifty cents to read it, puts the market cost of processing email messages at one dollar (Liebeskind, 1998). Therefore, it would seem that the cost of a letter is the highest, followed by a phone call, then an email, with a text chat session being the least costly; see Table 11. (Call back buttons and talk buttons would presumably cost about the same as a telephone call.)

It has been said that an unhappy customer would go and tell five friends. Now with the advent of the internet they can just as easily share their frustrations with five thousand (Thorton, 1999a).

Table 11: Transaction Costs by Type of Contact

Contact Method	Contact Cost
Letter	$25
(Fax – assumed to be about the same as a letter)	
Telephone call	$3 to $9
(Call-back – assumed to be about the same as a phone call)	
(Talk buttons – assumed to be about the same as a phone call)	
Email	$ 0.50 to $18
Text chat	$1

The quality of leads which resulted when the web was used in conjunction with simultaneous communications to the contact center is greater than with a straight telephone call or simple email (see Table 12). Telephone inquiries produced quality leads in thirty-five percent of the cases, whereas with email inquiries the rate for quality leads dropped to a low four percent. Leads which were a result of viewing the web site while interacting with a call center agent resulted in fifty-five percent being classified as quality leads (Fleischer, 1998b).

Table 12: <u>Percentage of Quality Sales Leads</u>

Contact Method	Percentage
Email	4%
Telephone call	35%
Web-enabled (including web talk, web call back, and web text)	55%

One of the major obstacles e-commerce sites have is earning the trust of consumers. Dianne Porter reported that sixty-four percent of on-line customers, or almost two out of every three, are reluctant to trust a web site enough to make a purchase (Porter, 1999c). Even more troublesome is that only one to three percent of those visiting e-commerce web sites actually end up buying on-line; lack of support was given as a major reason for this (Read, 1999a). Joe Fleischer echoed this explanation, citing a Forrester Research study which found that the single greatest reason for repeat web-site purchases was "great customer service," (Fleischer, 1998a, p. 28). Adding a web-enabled contact center to a web site is vital in those instances where "the human touch" and visual aids are instrumental in closing sales (Riggs & Thyfault, 1999, p. 60).

Additionally, of those who do shop on-line, thirty-five percent said they would buy more if the sites had real-time links to call center personnel. Similarly, of those who visited sites, but did not buy, fourteen percent said they would buy on-line if they could communicate with live agents. Customer service then will be a key element to establishing trust and driving sales on e-commerce sites. Unfortunately, only seventy-four percent of on-line shoppers admit to being satisfied with the experience. Happily, one way in which a company can build and establish trust in their customers is by merely sending a quick email message confirming that the order was received (Read, 1999b).

With all of the excitement and the promising outlook for the web-enabled contact center, it is important to remember that the internet is only one avenue for customer access and interaction (Sweat, 1999). The traditional forms of call center access still do make up a majority of customer contact and therefore need to be given their proper attention. According to Steven Dresner, web-enabled call center services will not supersede toll-free calling anytime soon. Even so, by the year 2000 the Gartner Group projected that thirty-five percent of call center access will be from non-traditional technology. This includes contacts made via faxes, emails, and web sites (Dresner, 1998) which are "call-enabled" to facilitate quick and effective communication with the call center.

The Future for Call Centers

Scott Thorton enjoys talking about the future and shared a triad of disarming quotes: "Change is the only constant;" "The pace of change is...accelerating;" and "It is impossible to predict the future," (Thorton, 1999a, p. 9).

In similar fashion Doctor Anton painted an attention-grabbing and compelling vision of the future for the call center industry. As consumers place a heightened value on their time, the accessibility of businesses becomes an increasingly important characteristic and a determining factor in the decision-making process. Quite succinctly, Anton summarized this paradigm as "at any time, from anywhere, in any form, and for free," (Anton, 1999b, p. 1-3). Geotel's Volpe, supported this view, stating that in the future a company's success will hinge solely on their ability to meet the "information needs of each customer when and how the customer wants it." The focus will be on determining these needs and having the proper resources ready and available to meet them (Volpe, 1999, p. 92). Similarly, "callers are demanding that [call centers] waste zero time and "deliver the goods" immediately," (Sturdy, 1997, p. 33). They are also "demanding choices in how they are served," (Cleveland, 1999, p. 114). Anton continued, that as competition pushes both price and quality to an expected level of uniformity, the distinguishing quality and competitive edge becomes accessibility. Furthermore, he claimed that the return on investment for steps to "increase customer accessibly is seldom less than 100% in the first year" and becomes substantially greater when the lifetime buying potential of each customer is considered (Anton, 1999b, p. 1-4). Additionally, he predicts that by 2000, fully fifty percent of all customer contact will take place through call centers and over the internet. As such, "the call center has the potential for being [a] company's most potent weapon for maintaining long-term customer relationships,"

(Anton, 1999b, 1-3).

Peter Cochrane of BT's Research Laboratory was more futuristic as he envisaged a "three click, one second, no handbook world," where anything he wants can be found within three mouse clicks on his computer, will be displayed within one second, and will not require referring to a manual to learn how to do it (QueueTips, 1999c, p. 2).

More pragmatically, Peggy Moretti espoused a future where investing in people is of paramount importance. The new millennium will move TSRs from processing calls to becoming a "corporate ambassador." To achieve this they will require even more training and greater technological expertise (Reiners, 1999, p. 34). Thorton echoed these sentiments as he envisioned the future's biggest challenge as being to attract and retain employees who possess the requisite skill sets to successfully deal with information and to master technology. "We are on the brink of a major transformation in our industry" and the demand for skilled labor will require the establishment of "teleservices as a profession," (Thorton, 1999b, p. 67).

Stopping short of making pronouncements, IBM's Patricia Mitchell merely pointed out the forces at work which will drive change and reshape the call center as it is known today. These forces include: 1) an emerging global market, coupled with deregulation, 2) "the blurring of traditional industry lines and the emergence of new "stealth" competitors," 3) customers who are more demanding and knowledgeable, and 4) new and more options for customer access (Mitchell, 1998, p. 64).

Lou Volpe perceived an important technological focus for the future residing in the ability to provide both the customer's profile and transaction history to the agents in real time (Volpe, 1999). Gene Gray, of the American Teleservices Association, also claimed that technology will be the driving force shaping the future of the call center industry. Technology will drive a redefinition of how the telephone is used, as well as force call centers to better process any type of communication. Gray also addressed the poor public image of the industry, lamenting the media's propensity to paint the call center industry as an enemy of the consumer. He advocated a future "need to get the word out that teleservices is good for America," (Gray, 1999, pp. 92-96).

Ten trends for call centers were outlined by Bill Rose. Among them were an upsurge in outsourcing, increased options for a virtual call center, more mergers, and greater demands on staff. The complete list of items is in Appendix G.

Jay Wood proposed that the process of customer service is the area to focus on versus the technology of customer service. Toward that end, he asserted that call centers of the future must provide five critical processes: 1) multiple access options, 2) "personalized service," 3) the option for self-service, 4) a proactive mindset, and 5) multimedia options (Wood, 1997, p. 34).

Ron Charnock considered the future of call centers from the perspective of value chain theory. He sees the "physical value chains" of "call centers, stores, direct mail campaigns, and salespeople" meeting the "virtual value chains of the electronic, networked world." Consumers will access these virtual chains by using internet-enabled computers, interactive television, and personal digital assistants (1997, p. 34).

Electing to look five years into the future, Bill Durr outlined the industry as he envisions it will be in the year 2004. The internet will hasten the demise or "deconstruction of the ACD" and advance the combining of various disparate subsystems to yield "a multi-media, multi-format customer transaction processing center," (1999, p. 34). Text chat will have the same expectation of real-time consideration that phone calls do today. The biggest effort, however, will reside in the timely and effective processing of the growing volume of email messages. It is no wonder then that with all of this heady technological development, 2004 will still witness labor costs as a center's biggest expense. Automated email systems will help minimize this need for human involvement by searching for key words and sending out appropriately canned written responses, but still the need for human intervention will be paramount. Durr maintained that of the three elements of a contact center, "people, process, and technology" only the process will be left to improve as the best technology will already be in place and people will be in short supply. The critical process needing attention, therefore, will be coaching. Coaching will be the technique utilized to maximize the investment made in human resources. Lastly, he envisioned a continued need to maintain the critical balance between productivity and quality. However, quality will need to be quantified, measured, and tracked in order to meet the growing demands and expectations of customers (Durr, 1999, p. 36).

Doctor Jackson, when asked about the possible future obsolescence of call centers, stated emphatically that it will never happen. There will always be a need for call centers, she added, and regardless of the amount or level of technical advances, there will always be a need to staff the call centers with agents to provide that personal touch when serving callers (1998a).

Paradigm Shifts

Anytime, anywhere, any form, for free.
A three click, one second, no handbook world.
Waste zero time; deliver immediately.
Provide information how and when customer wants it.

Predictions

More demanding and knowledge customers.
50% of customer contact will be via call center/internet.
Demand for multimedia options and access.
More outsourcing.
Increase in virtual call centers.
Physical value chain meets virtual value chain.
Text chat will have real-time expectations.

Recommendations

TSRs will need to become corporate ambassadors.
Establish teleservices as a profession.
Develop a proactive mindset.
Focus on coaching to improve (TSR) process.

Figure 6. Future Call Centers Issues.

Conclusion

Although there was scant information to be found about telephone answering services, there was a wealth of literature about call centers. By carefully reviewing this information, a profile of noteworthy items can be developed for the call center and call center industry in contrast to the telephone answering service industry (see Figure 7). Anyone in the telephone answering service industry, wishing to evolve into a call center, can consider this overview with respect to their own business. Differences between their reality and the profile will suggest a path to follow and goals to set in order to become a call center.

Call Center Industry Overview

Much larger than TAS industry.
Industry has history of rapid growth.
Industry has excellent future projections.
Industry will change even more rapidly in the future.

Operation

Uses toll-free numbers for national client base.
24 x 7 operation is not yet a given.
Forty-eight percent have multiple locations.
Telecommuting is an option (but needs to be used more).
Centers are becoming web enabled.
Email "ACD" is being implemented.

Labor (compared to TAS industry).

More time is spent on training.

More money is spent on training.

Higher percentage of total expenses spent on labor.

Lower turnover (but still too high).

Fifty-two percent of training time is classroom.
Much higher occupancy rate.

Metrics

Call duration is much longer than TAS industry.
Service level is not quite as good as TAS industry.

Key Call Center Technologies

CTI – Computer-Telephony Integration

IVR – Interactive Voice Response

ACD – Automatic Call Distribution

Skills-based routing
Workforce management systems

Figure 7. Noteworthy Items Contrasting Call Centers to Answering Services.

CHAPTER 3: METHODOLOGY

Introduction

The literature review, in the previous chapter, looked at both the telephone answering service industry and the call center industry. While there was little printed material to be found about the telephone answering service industry, a vast array of information was discovered about the call center industry. Since the goal of this endeavor is to uncover methodologies to migrate from the former industry to the latter, the comparisons and contrasts between the two, do, in fact, allow one to infer many such tactics.

The Approach

This, however, was only a partial glimpse at the complete picture. To fill in the puzzle and uncover the missing pieces, a survey of industry participants was conducted. It was anticipated that the survey would capture the past situations, the present perspectives, and future anticipations of a cross-section of company leaders. Further, it was expected that these leaders' organizations would currently be at different points in the industry life cycle, as well as having advanced varying distances down the call center migration pathway. It was also noted that some respondents might have no desire to jump from one industry to another, being content to forever reside in the telephone answering service industry.

Collectively, all these responses were envisioned to be useful in helping to paint profiles of various subgroups of industry thought and position. This would allow conclusions to be drawn which would be useful to those interested in taking their telephone answering service to the next plateau, that of being a call center.

An easy-to-complete, multiple-choice survey was selected to explore the past recollections, present conditions, and future forecasts of each participant as it related to their business. This style of survey was elected, in large part, as a result of this author's prior experience with, and disappointment from, a different style of survey. That style employed open-ended questions. Two limitations were learned from using indefinite and unrestricted queries. The first frustration was that the content of the responses varied greatly, both in terms of quality and quantity, with some individuals replying by means of a single, spontaneous sentence fragment; others constructed well considered and insightful compositions, often spanning multiple pages. The other difficulty arose in the effort to code, quantify, and summarize responses. This task was imprecise at best and caused this researcher considerable agony over being able to properly account for and track each response with integrity and accuracy.

Using a structured or closed survey style would address and eliminate both of these impediments. While several types of constrained investigative approaches were considered, the multiple-choice technique was selected. It was judged to offer satisfactory flexibility to the participant, while at the same time, providing the greatest consistency of responses and a more objective measurement for the researcher. A multiple choice format also would allow the survey to be completed in a relatively short period time, which would be a benefit for those with time constraints, encouraging a greater response rate. This design would also be less daunting for those contributors who disdain writing or the effort that goes into it. Again, the result would be a greater propensity to participate in, complete, and return the survey.

Data-Gathering Method

Just as there are multiple survey formats, there are several ways in which the survey can be conducted. These include a telephone survey, a mail survey, a fax survey, an in-person survey, and more recently, an email survey.

A telephone survey is, given the nature of this topic, a most compelling option since it would in fact be done by a call center. Unfortunately, it would be an expensive and time-consuming proposition. Also, it would be highly unlikely that one could obtain an accurate and complete database of the industry, which would be required in order to determine who to call. A benefit of a telephone survey, however, would be that it could be completed relatively quickly. Also, in the event that a flaw was uncovered in the survey, mid-course corrections could be easily implemented, though doing so would, from a purely academic standpoint, impact the integrity of the survey results.

A mail survey would suffer from the same two limitations of a telephone survey, those being the expense involved and the lack of a good mail list to use. A mail survey would also take a great deal of time, waiting for the surveys to be mailed, received, read, responded to, and returned.

Since a fax transmission is essentially instantaneous, a fax survey would greatly cut down on the amount of time to disseminate and receive the survey. Also, it would be less costly than either the phone survey or the mail survey. The prime limitation was that the fax numbers of the industry participants were even more elusive than their main phone numbers or addresses. As such, conducting the survey completely by fax was not a viable option.

Conducting the survey in person would provide many benefits, including being able to answer questions and clarify intent. It would also likely increase the response rate, as it would be easier to obtain one's participation in person than it would be to do so from a distance. An obvious problem, however, would be the geographic dispersion of the participants. This basic fact rendered an in-person survey a ridiculous scenario. Even though conducting the survey could be attempted at the various industry meetings, where many prospects would be present at one place and at one time, this would still entail traveling to seventeen destinations, spanning the course of a year. Clearly, an in-person survey was not a viable alternative.

This left email. Email is fast and essentially free. Although it is not as ubiquitous as the telephone or regular mail, it would be fairly common among those in the telephone answering service and call center industries. The difficulty with email was, again, the unavailability of a database; one containing the email addresses of those in the industry. Even if such a list were available, email addresses change even faster than fax numbers.

Ultimately, the selected process was a combination of email and fax. Either technology could be used to distribute the survey and either medium could be used to receive the responses according to the preference of the participant. This would allow for the survey to be conducted in a timely manner while keeping the associated costs at a minimum.

The difficult hurdle remained in obtaining accurate and up-to-date lists of the fax numbers and email addresses for the target group. To address this, the various association sub-groups in the industry were tapped for assistance. Some of these groups have email list services; others have fax broadcasting capabilities, while many have newsletters. These sources were utilized to promote the survey and encourage participation.

Database of Study

It was determined that the only effective method of communicating the existence of the survey to the target audience was to seek the assistance of the existing industry user groups and associations. Each group has one or more established system of communicating with their constituency; these existing mechanisms could be used to seek participation in the survey.

In order to obtain the assistance and participation of each of these organizations, it was decided that something of value needed to be offered in return. Therefore, each industry group, which had a sufficient response rate from their members, would receive a survey profile of just their members. It was hoped that this would not only secure the groups' support and involvement, but also provide them with data which would be useful in serving their members.

Several of these groups had established email lists allowing their members to quickly and easily communicate with each other. Email lists are conceptually an electronic bulletin board, on which questions can be posted and responded to using the internet. All email intended for the group is sent to a single, specific email address. A computer receives this email and consequently sends it to everyone who has signed up for, or subscribed to, the list. This way every member can see all the postings and read each of the responses. Mail lists can be either open or closed. An open list allows anyone to sign up and participate; it is open to all. A closed list only allows members, or other authorized applicants, to join; it is closed to non-members. All of the groups' email lists in question are closed lists. There are at least six such lists in the industry, likely more.

Since one must be a member to subscribe to and join a closed list, only those organizations, with email lists, of which this author is a member could be used to promote the survey. This included four of the six known lists. An email communication was sent to each of these lists, soliciting assistance and participation. As a reward for participation, each respondent would be eligible to receive a summary of the compiled results; this was in addition to the benefit that the entire group would receive should the responses be sufficient to generate a group profile. The text of the message sent to each mail list is shown below in Figure 8; the complete email is included in Appendix G.

"Hello, I invite you to participate in a survey to measure past changes and project future trends within the industry.

"This survey is being conducted in connection with research for my Ph.D. dissertation, measuring the changing dynamics in the TeleServices/Call Center industry. All individual responses will remain confidential; only aggregate data will be shared and included in my dissertation.

"The survey is designed to be easy to complete and should take less than five minutes. To participate, call 616-553-xxxx from a fax machine or send an email request to dehaan@xxxxxxx.net; put "survey" in the subject line.

"Each participant will receive the compiled results of the survey. Each industry group, which has a measurable response, will receive a private summation of their members' surveys, contrasted to the industry as a whole.

"Please take a few moments to obtain and complete the survey so that you and your association can benefit from the results. We need a good response from each organization's members to be able to provide specific analysis for the group. Thank you"

Figure 8. Text of Email Soliciting Survey Participation.

At the same time, each user group and association was directly contacted, asking for their participation in promoting the survey to their constituents. A total of seventeen such groups were identified. Each group which had a known email address was sent the request in that format; six organizations were contacted in this manner. Then, each group with an identified fax number was faxed a request to participate; five organizations were contacted in this manner. Five groups had both known email addresses and fax numbers and were contacted by both methods. Lastly, one group, with neither an identified email address nor fax number, was mailed their request. The list of the groups and their method of contact are detailed in Appendix H. The text of the request is shown below in Figure 9, while a sample email is in Appendix I and a sample letter and fax (which used the same layout) follow in Appendix J.

It was hoped that groups would promote the survey to their members and encourage them to participate so that the group would receive a profile of their members. The groups had various means of communicating with their members, including newsletters, email, and fax broadcasting, as well as the above-mentioned email lists.

Regardless of how they learned about the survey, those individuals who wished to take part could indicate their interest by sending a request to this author's email or calling a fax-on-demand number. If they responded via email, the survey would be sent back by email as an attached file, along with brief instructions, as shown in Figure 10.

"I invite (insert group name) members to participate in a trade survey to measure past changes and project future trends within the industry.

"This survey is being conducted in connection with research for my Ph.D. dissertation, measuring the changing dynamics in the TeleServices/Call Center industry. All individual responses will remain confidential; only aggregate data will be shared and included in my dissertation.

"The survey is designed to be easy to complete and should take less than five minutes. To participate, your members can call 616-553-xxxx from a fax machine or send an email request to dehaan@xxxxxxx.net; put "survey" in the subject line.

"Each participant will receive the compiled results of the survey. Each industry group, which has a measurable response, will receive a private summation of their members' surveys, contrasted to the industry as a whole.

"Please share this opportunity with your members and encourage them to participate. We need a good response from your members to be able to provide you with a specific analysis of your organization.

"If you have any questions about this, please call me. Thank you, Peter L. DeHaan"

Figure 9. Text of Email to User Groups and Associations.

"Thank you for your willingness to participate in my Ph.D. survey. It is attached in a Word 6.0 file.

"(If you are not able to read it, please let me know and I can resend it as a Word Perfect file, a text file, or include the survey in the body of the email.)

"The survey should take less than 5 minutes to complete, so why not do it right away? When you are finished, fax it to 616-553-xxxx.

"Again, thank you for your assistance."

Figure 10. Email Instructions for Completing the Survey.

Alternatively, interested parties could call the fax-on-demand system from their fax machine and receive the survey by fax. In the case of receiving the survey by fax, no additional instructions were provided, other than what were included with the actual survey. In either event they were asked to return the completed survey by fax (though some choose to do so via email).

Survey Design

The survey was divided into three sections to reflect the respective time frames for which information was sought. These sections were labeled as "A Look at the Past" (questions one through four), "A View of the Present" (questions five through eleven), and "Plans for the Future" (questions twelve through sixteen). Three questions were repeated in each section, one seeking a descriptive label to be applied to the respondent's organization, the second asking for major concerns, and the third requesting the greatest concern; all of these three questions were repeated for each of the time frames in question. In addition, the first section, which addressed the past, asked for the year the organization or division was founded (question one). The second section, which looked at the present, also contained additional items about how things had changed in recent years (questions five through eight). The third section, which anticipated what lies ahead, asked for input on overall direction for the future (questions fifteen and sixteen). The survey concluded with two profile questions (seventeen and eighteen) and two optional questions (nineteen and twenty). The profile questions asked the respondents' title or position and also their tenure in the industry. The optional questions solicited which user groups and industry associations they belonged to and if they wished to receive a summary of the results of the survey. Altogether, there were twenty questions included in the survey.

While all of the items in the survey were included for a specific reason and purpose, the foundation of the survey was those three portions which were repeated in each section. The first one sought to have the respondent place a descriptive label on their organization, asking them to pick "a telephone answering service," "a teleservices company," or "a call center." No definitions were given for any of these three terms, and it was left to each individual to assign the meaning they felt appropriate. The purpose of this question was to determine if the organization had changed, or would be changing, its focus over time or if their direction was constant. Therefore, the participant's definition of these terms, whatever they might be, would be irrelevant in correctly providing the desired tracking data. This was done in questions two (past), nine (present), and twelve (future).

The next repeated question asked the respondents to identify major concerns their organization faced during each of these time frames. An identical list of items was repeated with each version of the question. The items, which numbered nineteen, were grouped into four categories: TSR issues, sales and marketing issues, technical issues, and financial issues, effectively covering all aspects of the organization. (Administrative issues were intentionally omitted because, if they were selected, it would be a direct and negative reflection on the individual completing the survey; as such it was thought that any results in this area would be inconclusive.) This query was repeated in questions three (past), ten (past), and thirteen (future).

The final query, which was repeated, was done so in questions four (past), eleven (present), and fourteen (future). It simply stated, "on the previous question, circle the most important concern." The complete survey was four pages long and is shown in its entirety in Appendix K. The survey concluded with the following note of gratitude, "Thank you for being part of this research. Your time and input is greatly appreciated."

Once drafted, the survey was given to selected individuals, within the industry but with no connection to this effort, for review, evaluation, and testing. Their feedback was incorporated into a revised survey and the procedure repeated. It was believed that this effort would produce a survey which would garner the desired results in a clear and consistent manner.

Validity of the Data

It was requested that all surveys be returned by fax. As each survey was returned (which began within minutes after the first batch of surveys were sent out via email) it was put in proper order and the pages stapled together. Each survey was numbered sequentially, in the order it was returned, and placed into a three-ring binder. A few clever individuals returned their surveys by email. When this occurred, the surveys were printed, and the same procedure was applied to them.

The responses were then entered into a spreadsheet for easy tallying and sorting. The spreadsheet used was Microsoft Excel 97, SR-2, which was run on a Toshiba laptop, model Tecra 510CDT. This, incidentally, was the same computer used to send and receive the emails (using Microsoft Outlook 98) and to compose the survey, draft the letters, and compose this dissertation (Microsoft Word 97, SR-2). All of the above were stored on the computer's hard disk drive (along with supplemental backups), transferred to a floppy diskette, and copied to a networked file server, which was subsequently backed up to magnetic tape.

All surveys which were returned were processed in this manner. One, however, was missing a page due to a fax transmission error and thus was not able to be included or considered. The returned surveys were also reviewed to confirm that they were plausibly from industry sources and therefore contained relevant and trustworthy information. All responses were in fact deemed to be from industry participants and therefore suitable for and applicable to this course of study.

Originality and Limitations of the Data

Timelines in technology-based industries, such as the Telephone

Answering Service and Call Center Industries, are compressed. This implies that any research information gained has the inherent characteristic of possessing a relatively limited time span in which it is useful. Fortunately, due to the nearly instantaneous transmission afforded by the email and fax communications used for this survey, the value of the results was nevertheless assured. As such, the originality of the data gathered should be considered to be significant, untainted by time or unduly influenced by other participants or industry members.

Conversely, in any research survey there are inherent limitations, and the careful student of this work would be well advised to consider these before applying any conclusions. First, consider the method of dissemination and collection. All industry members who were neither on one of the four email lists nor a member of a participating group were not even presented with an opportunity for involvement. Although it was possible they could have heard about the survey from someone else, it was unlikely that this would happen with much frequency, if at all. Therefore, a significant portion of potential contributors were left out. One will be left to ponder if their feedback would have significantly altered the results of the survey or added any additional clarification.

Next, consider technical difficulties which could have blocked or frustrated one's involvement. First, examine email. There is nothing to guarantee that once an email message is sent that it will actually make it to its intended destination. While email is considered to be generally reliable and dependable, it is not infallible. At any point in the process, an email could be delayed or lost. This would apply to the initial participation request (some might have never gotten it), the response to participate (likewise with the potential for misfortune), the actual survey being sent via email (the survey as an attachment to the email presented the additional potential for human mishandling or confusion), and the email sent to the various user groups and associations.

A second area of technical concern exists in faxing. The sending machine might not send a legible image, the receiving machine could jam, the fax could have been received but misplaced, or multiple pages could have stuck together as they were faxed (this did indeed happen to one survey response, and it could not be used). These faxing issues could apply to both the sending and receiving of the survey, as well as to the communication with the user groups and associations. While these, and other technical problems, were not anticipated to be noteworthy, some of them could be more likely to occur with less technical people or those using older equipment. Again, the impact of such an occurrence on the response rate and ensuing results needs to be considered.

A significant limitation was on the survey itself. It was designed by this researcher to uncover a specific set of data in a preconceived direction. If that direction were faulty, the survey respondents would likely be unable to expose this, as the multiple-choice format was rigid in that regard. Alternatively, consider if the overall direction of the survey was in fact correct, but with important options left off of the survey. Since, by design, there was no provision for additional comment, contributors had no mechanism for communicating any omission. Although the survey did undergo independent testing, it was conceivable that both testers and researcher might have missed critical items.

Lastly, consider that the biggest variable and most limiting factor exists in the participants themselves. Did they read and understand the directions? Did they follow the directions? Did they answer every question? Did they take the survey seriously? Each of these questions needs to be asked for all of the responses on every survey. It should be assumed that all of these issues did indeed occur on at least one of the surveys, but which ones, how many, and how often? Since there was no way to judge the legitimacy of the responses, the only course of action was to equally include them all, with the hope that the majority were worthy of consideration and the minority, which were not worthy, did not significantly alter the results of the survey.

Summary

Every effort was made to develop a good, fair, accurate, and straightforward survey. Correspondingly, the effort was made to disseminate it to as many varied sources in the industry as possible in order to achieve the widest achievable participation. It is the belief of this author that these goals were accomplished with both tenacity and integrity, allowing the results of this effort to be accurate, dependable, and useful.

CHAPTER 4: DATA ANALYSIS

Introduction

This chapter deals with the analysis of the data gathered as a result of the survey. A review of the survey dissemination and collection procedure will be covered first, followed by a profile of the typical or average survey participant. Next, will be a summary of the survey's results. Since the survey was designed to compare and contrast past experiences with present practices and future plans, this section will, in and of itself, suggest future actions to consider.

After looking at the survey results as a whole, it was divided into subsets, allowing for comparisons between contrasting profiles, such as those who will change their businesses' direction to become call centers versus those who will not and those who already were a call center contrasted to those who were not. This effort will provide even more astute action items to consider. The most significant findings will then be compiled and summarized. The results of this will be a plethora of possible directions and actions to be considered and contemplated in order to develop a recommendation to migrate from a telephone answering service to a call center.

Survey Overview

As previously mentioned, the survey was essentially a closed-ended format which allowed participants to select from a list of provided answers (though a few questions did require short answers). This approach was done to encourage participation since it would not take too much of the contributor's time to complete and return the form. The survey had a total of twenty questions. The first eight items looked at the past; three addressed the present; and five anticipated the future. Of the final four elements, two sought participant profile information and two were optional, applying only to those participants who wished to receive the survey results.

Survey participants were solicited by sending email messages to several industry email lists. To support and supplement this effort, letters were sent to seventeen industry associations and user groups asking them to encourage their members to participate. The list of these groups and their method of contact are detailed in Appendix I.

Those who were interested in participating could reply to the email message and get the survey returned in the same manner. Alternatively, they could call a fax-on-demand system to receive the questionnaire via fax. The initial email solicitation request was sent on November 8, 1999, and the letters to industry groups followed on November ninth through twelfth.

Interested individuals responded within minutes from when the email request for participation was sent; replies continued for several weeks. The final participation request was received on December 3, 1999. All email messages were responded to within twenty-four hours. This was accomplished by sending the survey form as a file attachment via email. A total of sixty-four individuals responded via email and another fourteen called the fax-on-demand system. Assuming that no participant obtained their survey from both email and fax, a total of seventy-eight survey requests were received.

Once participants had completed their survey, they were instructed to fax it back. The first completed survey was returned on November 10, 1999, and the final one was received on December 10, 1999. Though most were returned via fax, as instructed, five individuals elected to reply to the email address from which the blank survey form was sent.

Altogether forty-seven surveys were returned, though two were unusable. One of the unusable surveys was missing a page as a result of faxing problems; the other unusable submission did not use the prescribed format, rendering their essay-style answers too difficult to accurately quantify and interpret.

The forty-seven responses compared to the original seventy-eight interested parties resulted in a sixty percent response rate. (The size of the industry audience was not possible to determine, but it was speculated that approximately five hundred individuals were exposed to the survey request. This projection results in roughly a ten percent overall response rate.)

Appendix M lists the dates of key survey activities and outcomes.

Analysis of Participants

As mentioned, some of the survey questions were designed to develop a profile of the respondents. Of the forty-five respondents, thirty-four (seventy-six percent) were the leaders of their organization, with titles such as President, CEO, and Owner. Ten surveys (twenty-two percent) were completed by individuals in operations management, such as those in the positions of Operations Manager, Vice President of Operations, Director of Operations, and General Manager. One participant (two percent) was a Sales Manager. This is shown in Table 13.

Table 13: Position Profile

Position	Percentage
Head of Organization	76%
Operations Management	22%
Sales Management	2%

In total, these forty-five respondents had an average industry tenure of 15.9 years which ranged from a high of forty years' experience to a low of two years.

Their respective companies were founded from between 1931 (sixty-eight years old) and 1992 (seven years old), with a mean of 1970. This equated to an average age of the participant's companies of twenty-nine years. Since the average age of the participants was less than the average age of their organizations, it was concluded that many respondents were not, in fact, the founder of their organization. Table 14 summarizes these figures.

Table 14: Tenure Profile

Position	High	Low	Mean
Organization's Age	68	7	29.0
Years of Experience	40	2	15.9
Difference	28	5	13.1

All but one individual wanted to receive the results of the survey. This equated to ninety-eight percent who expressed interest and suggested that offering to share the survey results was a motivator for participation.

Lastly, was the issue of membership in various industry groups. (Another participation incentive was that industry groups with a sufficient response would receive a group profile.) ATSI was most represented at thirty-six percent. NAEO followed a close second at thirty-four percent. (The author is a member and board representative of both ATSI and NAEO.) Rounding out the top three was CAM-X at nine percent. These three organizations will receive a profile of their members' responses contrasted to the rest of the group. (See Appendix Q for the survey results for these three industry groups.) Altogether, eleven groups were mentioned in the survey. (Note that many participants were members of more than one group.) Sadly, seven of the groups solicited by letter to participate were not mentioned at all. However, one group, IVMA, which was unknown to the author, and therefore not contacted, did have two members participate. These participants learned of the survey through other groups with were contacted.

The details of participation by group are listed in Appendix N.

Analysis of Survey

The remaining sixteen elements of the survey addressed the participants' recollection of the past, perception of the present, and anticipation for the future. Key among this was identifying and ranking their concerns for each period of time.

A total of nineteen issues of concern, grouped into four categories, were presented to participants. The four categories were TSR (staffing) issues, sales and marketing efforts, technology concerns, and financial worries. As a group, staffing concerns ranked as the top response for all three time frames with thirty-three percent (past), forty-one percent (present) and thirty-eight percent (future). Sales efforts were consistently ranked second for each era, with technological issues third, and financial fourth; refer to Table 15.

Table 15: <u>Concerns by Category</u>

Category	Past	Present	Future
TSR (staffing)	33%	41%	38%
Sales	26%	28%	29%
Technical	24%	22%	23%
Financial	17%	10%	10%

Although there was a consistent pattern for all categories among each time frame, the focus of the specific issue did shift for each time period. When analyzing the specific issues, the greatest concerns in the past were finding TSRs and affordable marketing, each at seven percent. For the present, the trepidation shifted to keeping TSRs, at nine percent, followed by finding TSRs and hiring sales staff, each at eight percent. At issue for the future was hiring sales staff (nine percent), trailed by finding TSRs and keeping TSRs, both at eight percent. This is detailed in Table 16 which shows the responses to each concern.

Table 16: <u>Detail of Concerns</u>

Category	Past	Present	Future
Finding TSRs	5%	8%	8%
Training TSRs	7%	5%	4%
Keeping TSRs	6%	9%	8%
Compensating TSRs	4%	5%	6%
Scheduling TSRs	3%	6%	4%
Dealing with Staffing Issues	4%	7%	7%
Hiring Sales Staff	5%	8%	9%
Training Sales Staff	3%	4%	3%
Keeping Sales Staff	1%	3%	4%
Providing Sales Compensation	1%	3%	3%
Finding Effective Marketing	6%	7%	6%
Affording Marketing	7%	3%	4%
Understanding Technology	6%	6%	6%
Finding Technology	5%	4%	5%
Affording Technology	5%	7%	7%
Installing/Maintaining Technology	5%	5%	4%
Keeping Financial Records	5%	2%	1%

Complying w/ Government Rules	5%	4%	4%
Obtaining Financing	6%	3%	4%

In studying the list of concerns, it can be seen that there was greater variation in the responses when comparing the past to the present (up to four percentage points of variation) then when contrasting the present to the future (no more than one percentage point difference). This would suggest that past changes were easier to identify than future changes were to forecast. Nevertheless, there were five trends which did result. Three items were shown to have increased in importance over time, while two tendencies exhibited a decrease in importance.

The three issues which demonstrated a trend of increasing concern were compensating TSRs, hiring sales staff, and keeping sales staff. Inadequate TSR compensation was identified in the literature search as an industry weakness. Inadequate compensation can lead to retention problems, especially during times of low unemployment, thereby impacting the quality of service and consistency of delivery. Keeping or retaining TSRs showed a big increase from the past to the present (thereby tracking with an increase in concerns over TSR compensation issues), but was expected to decrease slightly in the future, suggesting that it was anticipated that efforts to increase compensation will have a future positive impact on retention.

Hiring sales staff was the second trend of increasing importance, incidentally it ended up as the most mentioned future concern. Coupled with this was the retention of sales staff. These two items worked in tandem and tracked an industry trend for increased marketing. The days of the reactive-style, order-taking approach to garner new clients are over and are being replaced with a more organized, proactive sales effort. As such, it was no wonder that hiring and retaining sales staff did take on greater attention. This tracks with the increasing trend found in the overall category of sales (see Table 15).

The issues which did present and will present less anxiety were training TSRs and keeping financial records. The explanations for both were easy to infer. Training TSRs has been such a big issue in the past (tied as the top concern) that many industry groups have offered much in the way of content and support to assist their members in effectual training. Chief among these efforts was a series of interactive CD-ROM training programs developed by ATSI over the past three years. It was likely that these efforts were effective and therefore lessened training worries. The issue of reduced attention to keeping financial records was likely a result of an industry which became more sophisticated, therefore rendering this less of an issue. Correspondingly, those industry players which did not make this transition were arguably more likely to have gone out of business or to have been acquired.

A third and final methodology of considering the database of concerns was to chart the top response within each category. Again, there was greater variation between past and present than between present and future, nevertheless, the results were instructive. For future concerns, the top TSR issue was finding TSRs. Correspondingly, the leading sales issue was hiring sales staff. For the technology category, the main problem was affordable technology, while the financial category's greatest worries were complying with government regulations and obtaining financing. The results for the present were quite similar. They were keeping TSRs (TSR category), hiring sales staff (sales issues), affording technology (technology), and complying with government rules and regulations (finance group). The most common concerns for the past (by category) were more illustrative. They were training TSRs, affording marketing, understanding technology, and obtaining financing. The leading concern for each category is summarized in Table 17.

The preceding analysis was of the sections in the survey where respondents could select as many answers as they wished. The results were somewhat different when they were asked to focus on the single most important concern. (In some cases respondents were unable or unwilling to give a single answer and reported multiple "greatest concerns." In these instances a single point was divided among each response. This was deemed as the best way to consider their input while retaining the integrity of the results.)

When viewed this way, the top five concerns in the past were obtaining financing (twenty percent), affording marketing (ten percent), and at eight percent each, keeping TSRs, compensating TSRs, and finding effective marketing.

Table 17: <u>Most Common Concern for Each Category</u>

Category	Past	Present	Future
TSR (staffing) .	Training TSRs	Retaining TSRs	Finding TSRs
Sales .	Affording Marketing	Hiring Sales Staff	Hiring Sales Staff
Technical .	Understanding Technology	Affording Technology	Affording Technology
Financial ' .	Obtaining Financing	Complying w/ Regulations	Complying w/ Regulations & Obtaining Financing

Although there were some major shifts when moving forward in time to the primary present issues, there were also some reoccurring themes. The most substantial current issues facing the respondents were finding TSRs (nineteen percent), keeping TSRs (eleven percent), finding effective marketing (nine percent), training TSRs (eight percent), and hiring sales staff (eight percent).

For the future, there were again new concerns which surfaced, as well as familiar issues. Two responses tied for first for the most important future concern; they were keeping TSRs and understanding technology, both at fourteen percent. Next, was finding TSRs (eleven percent), then hiring sales staff (ten percent), and last finding technology (nine percent).

Only one item appeared on the top five for all three categories; it was keeping TSRs. All answers are shown in Table 18.

From this list (Table 18), six concerns showed a consistent trend of increasing in importance over time, while only one steadily decreased in emphasis over time; the rest did not have a reliable trend. Ranked in order of their magnitude of change, the issues which increased in importance over time were understanding technology, finding technology, keeping TSRs, hiring sales staff, installing and maintaining equipment, and affordable technology. It is noteworthy that four of the six items were technology issues. This suggests an important future trend. The only concern which showed a steady decline in importance over time was training sales staff.

Table 18: Most Important Concern

Category	Past	Present	Future
Finding TSRs	7%	19%	11%
Training TSRs	5%	8%	8%
Keeping TSRs	8%	11%	14%
Compensating TSRs	8%	3%	3%
Scheduling TSRs	2%	6%	3%
Dealing with Staffing Issues	4%	3%	3%
Hiring Sales Staff	7%	8%	10%

Training Sales Staff	4%	3%	0%
Keeping Sales Staff	1%	0%	0%
Providing Sales Compensation	1%	0%	0%
Finding Effective Marketing	8%	9%	3%
Affording Marketing	10%	0%	0%
Understanding Technology	1%	7%	14%
Finding Technology	1%	6%	9%
Affording Technology	2%	3%	4%
Installing/Maintaining Technology	1%	2%	4%
Keeping Financial Records	6%	2%	3%
Complying w/ Government Rules	4%	4%	8%
Obtaining Financing	20%	3%	4%

When the most important concerns were grouped by category, two remarkable trends emerged. First was that sales issues as major concerns decreased over time, from thirty-one percent (in the past) to twenty-one percent (for the present), to twelve percent (in the future). Conversely, the technology category showed a substantial increase over time from a low of four percent in the past, to nineteen percent for the present, peaking at thirty-two percent for the future.

The TSR and financial groups did not show a consistent trend over time. All of these results are shown in Table 19.

Table 19: <u>Most Important Concerns by Category</u>

Category	Past	Present	Future
TSR (staffing)	34%	51%	40%
Sales	31%	21%	12%
Technical	4%	19%	32%
Financial	30%	9%	16%

Survey participants were asked to identify a label for their organization. For this question, a definite trend emerged. When looking at the past, 93.3 percent viewed their company as a telephone answering service. At present they considered themselves to be a teleservices company (42.2 percent), whereas in the future nearly half planned on being a call center (46.7 percent). A summary of all answers is shown below in Table 20.

Table 20: <u>Participant's Organization</u>

Category	Past	Present	Future
Telephone Answering Service	93.3%	28.9%	15.6%
Teleservices Company	4.4%	42.2%	37.8%
Call Center	2.2%	28.9%	46.7%

Four questions were geared at tracking changes in the size and scope of activity within the participant's organization. While the results did not suggest any future action to be considered, they were nonetheless encouraging in that they showed that the respondents' organizations overall had more accounts, greater revenue, more calls, and longer calls than in the past. This is shown in Table 21.

Table 21: <u>Changes Over the Past Few Years</u>

Result	Number of Accounts	Revenue	Number of Calls	Length of Calls
Increased greatly	36%	42%	38%	20%
Increased somewhat	32%	42%	33%	36%
Stayed the same	11%	7%	16%	29%
Decreased somewhat	14%	4%	7%	16%
Decreased greatly	7%	4%	7%	0%

The final two questions addressed future plans. The first was to identify possible courses of action for the organization and the second was to pick the most likely option. The strategies which would be pursued were to increase sales and marketing efforts (forty-nine percent), pursue acquisitions (twenty-six percent), position the business to be sold (twelve percent), scale back the business (seven percent), and lastly to maintain the business as is (five percent).

When forcing participants to select a primary course of action, the results became more focused. Increasing sales and marketing was foremost (at fifty-nine percent), followed by pursue acquisitions (seventeen percent), scale back and maintain as is (both at ten percent), and position the business to be sold (five percent). See Table 22.

Table 22: <u>Future Plans</u>

Strategy	All Answers	Most Likely
Scale back business	7%	10%
Position it to be sold	12%	5%
Maintain business as is	5%	10%
Pursue acquisitions	26%	17%
Increase sales and marketing	49%	59%

These main observations and key survey results are summarized in Figure 11.

TSR concerns

Overall, TSR issues cause the most future concern
Retaining TSRs is the key current concern.
Finding TSRs is a lessor, but vital current and future concern.
Keeping TSRs is the key future issue.
There is now less concern about training TSRs.
Compensating TSRs in a trend of growing importance.

Sales concerns

Decreased overall concern about sales (except for hiring).
Hiring sales staff is and will be the key concern.
Concern for hiring sales staff is a trend of growing importance.
Retaining sales staff is another trend of increasing concern.

Technology concerns

Increased overall concern about technology issues.

Understanding technology will be the future key concern.

Growing concern over being able to afford technology.
High future concern for finding the right technology.

Financial concerns

Overall financial concerns will increase.

Some concern about financing and complying with regulations.
Less concern about record keeping.

Future Plans

Growth via sales and marketing is leading direction.

Growth via acquisition is a secondary plan.
Much divergence in future plans and options.

Figure 11. Overview of the Survey Analysis.

Survey Subsets

While the analysis of the survey as a whole was both enlightening and instructive, additional value was gleaned by examining various subgroups of the surveys. In each case, a key subset was identified, and the results of those surveys were generated. Then the remaining surveys (those not selected for the subset) were similarly processed so as to form a contrasting picture. By comparing the two subgroups, key differences could be identified and examined, each of which shed additional illumination of the emerging picture of turning a telephone answering service into a call center.

While many database subsets were considered, four were seriously evaluated. First, was those who planned to become call centers in the future. This group of respondents tracked precisely with the purpose of this study. The findings which resulted from the analysis of this subset were both insightful and enlightening.

The second subgroup considered was an extension of the future call center subset. It was those who planned to become either a call center or a teleservices company in the future. The results garnered from this group were inconclusive, in part paralleling the future call center subset, but frequently diverging. In fact, the historical statistical results from this group were not as good as the control group. As such, it was determined that this cross-section of the database did not have any beneficial contribution to the study and the results were therefore not reported.

The third subset considered was those respondents who were currently running a call center. Statistically, this group was superior to any other cross-section of the database. The insight gained from this group further supplemented the conclusions from the first subset and provided additional clarity and profundity since they had progressed further on the learning curve.

The final subset, which was considered, was a broadening of the third and included present teleservice companies as well as present call centers. It was found that this group mirrored the conclusions of the third group but were not as pronounced. As such there was no reason to repeat these previous findings; therefore, this subset was also not covered herein.

Subset of Future Call Centers

The first, and potentially most useful, subset of surveys considered was the one that planned to become a call center in the future. This group's intentions paralleled this course of investigation and study.

When this group was asked to identify their most important future concern, they indicated it was retaining TSRs (sixteen percent), whereas the control group's main future focus was on finding TSRs (eighteen percent). Interestingly, these items were both groups' primary present concerns, as well. Secondary concerns of the subset of future call centers were hiring sales staff, understanding technology, and complying with government regulations (all at twelve percent). The only other noteworthy future concerns were obtaining financing (eight percent) and adequate record keeping (seven percent). These are summarized in Table 23.

Table 23: <u>Key Future Concerns for Future Call Centers</u>

Concern	Percentage
Keeping TSRs	16%
Hiring sales staff	12%
Understanding technology	12%
Complying with government rules and regulations	12%
Affording technology	8%
Obtaining financing	8%
Keeping financial records	7%

When asked to list all future concerns, the results were less pronounced and more vast. The top responses were hiring sales staff, finding TSRs, keeping TSRs, finding technology, and affording technology, followed by compensating TSRs.

The issue of finding effective marketing promotions provided another area of dissimilarity. Within the subset of future call centers, only one percent identified it as a present key concern, while the control group listed it as their second greatest concern at fifteen percent. For the future it dropped to zero for the subset and five percent for the control group. Interestingly, although sales and marketing issues were not ranked as major concerns, this subset's future plan was, in fact, to focus on sales and marketing efforts (seventy-two percent) versus forty-eight percent for the control group.

Overall, future financial issues ranked higher (twenty-eight percent) among the subset than the control group (five percent). Whereas overall future technology concerns were higher in the control group (forty percent) than the subset (twenty-two percent).

Lastly, the historical statistical data was analyzed. The percentage of companies which experienced an increased number of calls in the past few years was identical for both groups (seventy-one percent). However, companies in the subset were slightly less likely to see an increase in the number of accounts (sixty-seven percent versus sixty-nine percent), but more likely to experience an increase in revenue (ninety percent compared to seventy-nine percent). The subset was also more likely to observe an increase in the length of time per call (seventy-two percent compared to forty-two).

In conclusion, the data from the subset of future call centers suggested that they were fairly comfortable finding TSRs and but were concerned about retaining TSRs. Likewise, they were content with their sales and marketing efforts – which was also their future focus. They placed greater emphasis on financial issues (possibly because they recognized a greater need) but were less concerned about technology issues (likely because they already understood or possessed it). Staffing issues remained dominant but were not as significant. They had already begun a shift to having fewer accounts, which produced more revenue with the same amount of work (the same number of calls). These conclusions are listed in Figure 12.

- Need to better retain TSRs.

- Staffing issues will remain dominant, but not as significant.

- Need to be able to hire suitable and effective sales staff.

- Maintain expertise in sales and marketing.

- Need to better understand technology.

- Financial issues will take on increasing importance.

- Affording technology and obtaining financing are concerns.

- Future direction will be growth through sales and marketing.

Figure 12. Overview of the Subset of Future Call Centers.

Subset of Existing Call Centers

This next subset of surveys was those who had already become a call center. The significance with this group was that they have already achieved what this work endeavors to uncover. As such, their current concerns were a relevant consideration, while their future worries provided more in-depth and far-reaching input.

In this group their key future concern was, again, keeping TSRs (sixteen percent). A secondary concern was affording technology (thirteen percent); the call centers' other main concerns were compliance with government rules and regulations (eleven percent), hiring sales staff (ten percent), and understanding technology (ten percent). All of the noteworthy future concerns are shown in Table 24. Note that of the ten issues listed, seven were employee related.

Table 24: <u>Key Future Concerns for Existing Call Centers</u>

Future Key Concerns	Percentage
Keeping TSRs	16%
Affording technology	13%
Complying with government rules and regulations	11%
Hiring sales staff	10%
Understanding technology	10%
Finding TSRs	6%
Training TSRs	6%
Properly Compensating TSRs	6%
Scheduling TSRs	6%
Dealing with TSR issues	6%

When considering their present key concerns, essentially the same issues were covered, though the order and priority did change. Their current key concerns were keeping TSRs (seventeen percent), finding TSRs (fifteen percent), and hiring sales staff (twelve percent). These are shown in Table 25.

When comparing the present concerns with future concerns,

finding TSRs will become much less important (from fifteen percent down to six percent) and hiring sales staff will become somewhat less important (twelve to ten percent). Conversely, complying with government rules and regulations will become increasingly more important (rising from zero to eleven percent) and understanding technology will increase somewhat in importance (eight to ten percent).

Table 25: <u>Key Present Concerns for Existing Call Centers</u>

Present Key Concerns	Percentage
Keeping TSRs	17%
Finding TSRs	15%
Hiring sales staff	12%
Affording technology	10%
Understanding technology	8%
Training TSRs	7%
Properly Compensating TSRs	7%
Scheduling TSRs	7%
Dealing with TSR issues	7%

When viewed by group, TSR and sales issues will present less concern in the future, whereas technical and financial issues will be cause for greater concern. Refer to Table 26 for details.

Table 26: <u>Call Center Concerns by Group</u>

Group	Current	Future
TSR (staffing)	60%	44%
Sales	19%	10%
Technical	19%	27%
Financial	2%	19%

The historical statistics of the existing call centers provided confirmation that migrating to a call center is a desirable outcome. Of the existing call centers, ninety-three percent saw their revenue increase in the past few years (none reported a decrease). This was the highest result of any subset. They also held a slight lead among those who witnessed an increase in their number of accounts (sixty-nine to sixty-eight percent). Seventy-seven percent had an increased number of calls (versus sixty-nine percent among the control group) and seventy-six (versus forty-seven) percent witnessed an increase in the length of calls.

For the future, eighty-three percent planned to make sales and marketing their primary goal while none intended to scale back their business or position it to be sold. Contrast this to forty-eight, fourteen, and seven percent respectively for the control group.

In conclusion, the data from the subset of existing call centers showed that they had done the best at achieving the results most businesses seek, that is, increasing revenue. All of the conclusions generated from the first subset of surveys, the future call centers, remained true for this group as well. Some items were less significant, while others were more pronounced. There were, however, two items which were not present in the prior group but did dramatically surface with this subset. With the future call center subset, the number of concerns attributed to sales and technology did not substantially change when comparing the present to the future. For the subset of existing call centers, a large shift did occur. Sales issues dropped in half, from nineteen percent down to ten percent, while technology concerns took a big jump, from nineteen percent to twenty-seven percent. This suggested that existing call centers were essentially comfortable with their sales and marketing prowess but expected rapid technological changes to cause the need for increased attention and focus on the future. These conclusions are shown in Figure 13.

- Need to better retain TSRs.

- Staffing issues will remain dominate.

- Still will need to be able to hire effective sales staff.

- Continue sales and marketing efforts.

- Need to better understand technology.

- Financial issues become somewhat more important.

- Affording technology is a great concern.

- Future direction will be growth through sales and marketing.

- Sales concerns will diminish overall.

- Technology concerns will increase overall.

Figure 13. Overview of the Subset of Existing Call Centers.

Significant Findings

Significant findings were garnered from both the analysis of the completed surveys as well as the scrutiny of various subsets. In regard to the survey as a whole, the array of future concerns provided a list of possible action items and suggested alternatives to consider in the effort to migrate from a telephone answering service to a call center. These included staffing issues (for TSRs, as well as sales staff), keeping up with technology (both comprehending and acquiring), future plans and options, and financial issues. Interestingly, aside from the staffing aspect of sales, there was no other significant sales and marketing trepidation.

Staffing anxieties formed the biggest block of both present and future concerns. Leading the pack were retaining TSRs, finding TSRs, and finding sales staff. Ancillary issues included compensating TSRs and retaining sales staff. There was now less concern voiced for training issues, assumedly because it was deemed to be under control.

Technology topics took on increased importance to the industry, with merely understanding technology rated as the top issue. Aside from that dilemma, there was the constant worry about being able to find the right technology. This was followed by a growing concern of being able to afford the desired technology once it is understood and found.

Survey participants had widely diverging views on future strategic options for their companies. While the goal to grow through sales and marketing was prominent, it was far from conclusive as some wanted to sell, a few would scale back, and others chose to maintain the status quo. Growth via acquisition was a common, but secondary, strategy.

A few noteworthy concerns surfaced in the area of finances. Financing one's business activities and complying with regulations were chief concerns. All of the main survey findings are summarized in Figure 14.

In similar fashion, the database of subsets offered additional action items and trends for consideration. For the subset of future call centers, there were many parallels, but also some key differences. For them, staffing concerns were again the dominant issue, however the focus was on two key areas, retaining TSRs and hiring sales staff. The implication was that this group could successfully navigate the difficult path of finding TSRs and was basically comfortable with compensating them and therefore their only concern was with keeping them. In similar fashion, this group statistically demonstrated a fair amount of comfort with their sales and marketing competence and needed to simply make sure there was adequate skilled staff to execute the existing marketing strategy.

- Need to find TSRs.

- Need to better retain TSRs.

- Need to find sales staff.

- Need to better compensate TSRs.

- Need to better retain sales staff.

- Need to better understand technology.

- Need to be able to find the right technology.

- Need to find a way to afford the needed technology.

- Need to understand and comply with rules and regulations.

- There exists no consensus on future strategy.

- Training TSRs is not an issue, but it must be maintained.

- Sales and marketing is not an issue, but it must be maintained.

Figure 14. Summary of Survey.

For this subgroup, they too needed to better understand technology, however they expressed less of a need to do so, but a greater fear about being able to afford it. Unlike the group as a whole, this subset had little concern with being able to find the right technology, which implied they were confident with their existing level of technological knowledge.

This subset of future call centers had the same overall low level of concern with sales issues as did the entire group, though their specific future focus was more heavily on hiring the right sales staff. Their future strategy was on growth through sales and marketing efforts, but it was the dominant direction for this group, with other options being much less substantial. The same heightened level of concern over regulation compliance also was evident. Refer to Figure 15 for a summary.

- Need to better retain existing TSRs.

- Maintain staffing expertise in hiring, training, scheduling, etc.

- Need to be able to hire effective sales staff.

- Maintain competence in sales and marketing.

- Affording technology is a great concern.

- Need to better understand technology.

- Concerned about complying with government regulations.

- Future strategy will be growth through sales and marketing.

Figure 15. Summary of Future Call Centers.

Lastly was the subset of existing call centers, which in most respects tracked with the future call centers. This group was equally concerned about retaining TSRs, which was their biggest worry. Their other top concerns were the same as for the future call centers, but none were as pronounced. These included hiring sales staff, affording technology, complying with regulations, and understanding technology. As such, virtually all tertiary concerns were given slightly more importance among this group. This suggested that their future outlook was more holistic and balanced than those who planned on becoming call centers.

Overall, this group envisioned that its degree of concern for sales issues would decrease in the future, whereas their concern about technology was expected to increase.

For this subset, they too had increased concern over technology issues, but not to the degree of the entire survey population. They expressed less of a need to understand it, but a greater worry about being able to afford it. Again, this suggested that they were further along the learning curve both in terms of understanding the technology as well as being cognizant of its cost. See Figure 16 for a summary of these findings.

- Need to better retain TSRs.

- Still will need to be able to hire effective sales staff.

- Affording technology is a great concern.

- Will need to comply with government rules and regulations.

- Need to better understand technology.

- Staffing issues will remain of paramount importance.

- Has high confidence and expertise in sales and marketing.

- Future direction will be growth through sales and marketing.

- Sales concerns will diminish overall.

- Technology concerns will increase overall.

Figure 16. Summary of Existing Call Centers.

The most encouraging finding from the survey was the vindication that the purpose of this dissertation does in fact offer a viable business strategy. The group of participants moving in the direction of becoming a call center had a greater likelihood of having recent increases in revenue, whereas the subset of companies who already were call centers showed the greatest probability of any subset for increased revenue. Clearly becoming a call center is a feasible and desirable strategy for a telephone answering service to adopt.

Conclusion

The results from the surveys provided a wealth of information. This will be used to advance plans to consider in developing a recommendation for turning a telephone answering service into a call center. The survey as a whole offered general suggestions for the future. The subset of future call centers forwarded more specific ideas, while the subset of existing call centers offered a set of current expectations, as well as being able to look further down the life cycle, thus rendering the most valuable insight. These items, coupled with the results of the literature search, will provide a wide array of options for consideration.

CHAPTER 5: SUMMARY

Introduction

The purpose of this research was to determine how to guide a telephone answering service into becoming a call center. The literature search, in chapter two, provided a vast array of information and insight into the current state and future expectations of the call center industry and contrasted it to the telephone answering service industry. This effort, which documented differences between the two industries, also implied several areas to be addressed when migrating from a telephone answering service to a call center.

The results of the survey, in chapter four, provided three sets of conclusions which also offered valuable input and insight. The first one provided an overview of the industry as a whole. The second assemblage looked at the subset of respondents who planned on being call centers in the future, while the third consideration was the subset of those who were now call centers. By contrasting these three findings, conclusions can be drawn as to what will currently need to be done to begin a telephone answering service's transformation into a call center, as well as what will be required in the future to fine-tune that effort. These observations will be put in context with conclusions from the literature search. Altogether, a road map will emerge to suggest a path to travel from answering service to call center.

The Basics

In contrasting the survey results as a whole to the two selected subgroups, two categories of observations emerged. The first was the key findings which were only relevant to the whole group, but not significant with either subset. These formed a baseline of essential characteristics critical for a telephone answering service interested in becoming a call center. The second group of understanding is best termed as universal truths; those items which were deemed critical regardless of survey cross-section and therefore applicable in all situations. These were key elements which should be highly regarded irrespective of future strategies or directions. Taken together these findings provide a platform on which the subsequent conclusions can be built.

There were five key discoveries found in the survey analysis of the entire group which were not present in the analyses of the subsets. These formed basic issues which since they were not present in the call center subsets were assumed to have been successfully addressed by that population. (An alternative conclusion considered was that these five items were not relevant to call centers, however a casual perusal of them confirmed that this was not a realistic conclusion). It should be noted that while all five of these items were concerns for the call center subsets, they were simply not major concerns.

The first was the need to find TSRs. This ranked as the second greatest concern overall and also the second major concern. Therefore, it was not only widespread, but it was also substantial. This issue took on much less importance with the call center subset, suggesting that it was a challenge they had successfully addressed and were comfortable dealing with.

The second concern paralleled the first, that being the issue of compensating TSRs. Again, it was concluded that this was an issue which the call center subset had satisfactorily dealt with, removing its status as a major concern for those sub-groups. There is also a connection between the two. Better compensation for TSRs makes it easier to attract candidates and subsequently to hire TSRs. It is therefore likely that by addressing the second item, the first is on its way towards resolution.

The third item was retaining sales staff. While this was not one of their top concerns, it did show a trend of increasing importance. This trend was not as pronounced with the subset of future call centers and did not exist at all with the subset of existing call centers (that is, they projected it would be less important in the future than in the present). Because of the steep learning curve for successful sales representatives, high turnover implies less efficacy with sales efforts and more unproductive time among sales staff.

Next, was a concern over being able to find the right technology. This ranked as the most important future concern for the respondents overall and though it was a concern for the call center groups, it was non-existent as a major concern.

The fifth observation of this section was that, overall, the participants had a divergence of future strategies, whereas the call center groups were quite focused on a strategy of growth via sales and marketing. This makes sense when considering that one whose future strategy is to scale back or maintain the business as is would not be interested in making an investment of time, money, and energy to turn it into a call center. In similar manner, positioning a business to be sold or a growth through acquisition strategy, while not mutually exclusive to forming a call center, are certainly strategies which would detract from efforts to become a call center. While it would be incorrect to conclude that if one's future strategy is not growth through sales and marketing that their vision is incompatible with becoming a call center, it would also be incorrect to deny a connection.

Two parenthetical issues were added to this list. These were items which were noteworthy due to the lack of concern demonstrated by the survey's participants. As a consequence, they were added to the list of basics in that a company struggling with these areas should similarly address them. These two items were TSR training and sales and marketing efforts. Both failed to register as major concerns and the implication was that they have been satisfactorily addressed.

All seven of these basics are listed in Figure 17.

- Need to develop an effective mechanism to find TSRs.

- Need to better compensate TSRs.

- There is a growing concern about retaining sales staff.

- More effort to find the right technology.

- Future strategy must be compatible with a call center push.

- Success in training TSRs must be maintained.

- Success in sales and marketing must be maintained.

Figure 17. The Baseline Essentials.

As previously mentioned, the survey also uncovered five items which were consistently and prominently present with each analysis. These were basic issues in that they seemed to exist as universal concerns. These common issues were to effectively retain TSRs, to find sales staff, to better understand technology, to be able to afford this technology once it had been found, and to comply with the growing number of government rules and regulations. These universal truths are listed in Figure 18.

- Need to develop ways to better retain TSRs.

- Need to be able to hire competent and successful sales staff.

- Need to be able to better understand technology.

- Need to determine how to afford the acquisition of technology.

- Need to confidently comply with rules and regulations.

Figure 18. Universal Truths.

The insight gained from the literature search suggested additional clarification of these basic issues by providing a composite view of the typical call center. The call center experiences much longer call duration than telephone answering services, uses toll-free numbers for a national reach, has an extensive investment in technology, boasts a higher occupancy rate for its TSRs (likely a result of greater economies of scale), and almost half were multiple location enterprises. Add to this list two distinctions of telephone answering services. These were that many call centers do not operate 24 x 7, whereas most telephone answering services do and the statistical fact that answering services have a slightly better service level. These are all summarized in Figure 19.

- Longer call duration.

- Uses toll-free numbers for a national reach.

- Intensive use of technology.

- Higher occupancy rates.

- Often multiple locations.

- Many are not 24 x 7.

- Could improve their level of service.

Figure 19. Call Center Overview
(compared to Telephone Answering Services).

Areas of Focus

The examination of the results gathered from the study of the two database subsets also resulted in worthwhile results. The first, those respondents who planned to become call centers in the future, matched the specific objective of this dissertation. As such, their particular issues have a direct correlation to the objective at hand. Even more valuable, however, was analysis of existing call centers. Their current concerns present items of future focus to the evolving telephone answering service, while their future concerns enable a more long-term vision to be established.

When looking at the conclusions and summary assembled from the subset of future call centers two items surfaced. The first was that they needed to maintain their focus on TSR issues, such as hiring, training, compensating, and scheduling. By doing so and attempting to raise their level of expertise to the next level, they will be that much closer to meeting the aforementioned universal concern of improving TSR retention. The second observation was that their future strategy will be principally to grow through maintaining their sales and marketing efforts. In essence, this can be summed up by saying that retaining TSRs is the key to providing the high level of service that call center clients expect and that without an intentional sales and marketing effort there will be a dearth of clients to serve.

More enlightening, however, were the implications of the subset of existing call centers. Here three tendencies were noteworthy. First, staffing issues will remain of paramount importance. Though this was true for the whole group, as well as the future call center subset, it was more apparent with this cross-section. In fact, when asked to state their most important future concern, forty-four percent responded with a TSR issue. The conclusions from the literature search provided a wealth of supporting information in this regard. First, was that TSRs will need to become a corporate ambassador. One of the ways in which this will be accomplished is by focusing on coaching to improve TSR skills. Next was training. Although the survey suggested that training was a past problem which has now been corrected, the literature search was unanimous in its assessment that more emphasis was needed on training. This included more time spent on training (over four weeks, about half of which would be classroom based), more money spent on training, budgeting more for staffing, and taking steps to reduce turnover (which was already much better for the call center industry than the telephone answering service industry).

Secondly, sales and marketing concerns will diminish in the future. In fact, it was thought to be only half as important for the future as it is for the present. This implied that they were confident in their ability for organizational promotion and client acquisition. When asked to identify their most important future concern, only one sales and marketing issue was even mentioned (hiring sales staff). This corresponded with the implication which resulted from the literature search, in which there was not a single mention of sales and marketing as it related to call centers. Truly, this does not seem to be an issue.

Thirdly, technology concerns will increase by almost fifty percent in the future. While finding the technology, as well as installing and maintaining it were not major concerns for call centers, understanding and affording the technology was a substantial cause for anxiety. The literature search concurred with the importance placed on technology, identifying five key call center technologies. They were computer-telephony integration, interactive voice response, automatic call distribution, skills-based routing, and workforce management systems. Add to this list of essentials the recommendations of becoming web-enabled, installing telecommuting technology, and eventually becoming a virtual call center.

These issues are summarized in Figure 20.

Maintain focus on TSR issues:

View TSRs as "corporate ambassadors."

Use coaching to improve skills.

Spend more time on training.

Invest more money in training.

Increase percentage of budget spent on staffing issues.

Take steps to further reduce turnover.
Offer telecommuting as an option.

Pursue growth via effective sales and marketing.

Maintain existing sales and marketing expertise.

Pursue technology:

Computer-telephony integration.

Interactive voice response.

Automatic call distribution.

Skills based routing software.

Workforce management systems.

Become web enabled.

Offer telecommuting.
Move toward becoming a virtual call center.

Figure 20. Areas of Focus.

To complete the picture, a profile of the future call center caller must be included. The call center of the future will have even more pressures on it than it does today. This will be in part because fifty percent of all customer contact is predicted to be through call centers and the internet and partly because of heightened caller expectations. As such, call centers will need to deal with customers who are more demanding and more knowledgeable. These callers will want information immediately and they will dictate when they will receive it and in what form. To address this, the call center will need to provide multimedia options and multiple points of access. These issues are shown in Figure 21, profile of call center callers.

While the establishment of basic call center issues (the baseline essentials and universal truths) and call center distinctiveness (the overview and focus) provided a compelling picture of what it takes to be a call center, there were also two seeming discrepancies between the survey analysis and the summary of the literature search. These were the issues of TSR compensation and TSR training and the actual degree of importance which should be assigned to them. In both cases the survey results suggested lesser importance, while the literature search addressed these issues with frequency and urgency.

- More demanding.

- More knowledgeable.

- Seeking instant response and satisfaction.

- Will dictate the time of the contact.

- Will dictate the form of the contact.

Figure 21. Future Call Center Callers.

TSR training was not on the radar screen of any of the survey analyses conducted. In fact, on the overall list of concerns it garnered only three to four percent mention, low enough to view it as being an insignificant issue. TSR compensation on the other hand was designated as one of the baseline essentials due to its high showing on the survey as a whole. However, when considering the call center subsets, it was downgraded in importance from a concern to merely a skill which needed to be maintained. The implication was that call centers had adequately dealt with compensation concerns. Contrast this to the emphasis which the literature search placed on improving TSR compensation for call centers and the results is incongruity.

There are three ways to deal with these apparent contradictions. One is to assume the survey findings are correct; the second is to trust the experts who were reported on in the literature search; and the third is to reconcile the dichotomy. This author will choose the latter by stating that the issues of training and compensation exist on a continuum. From the perspective of the survey participants, 93.3% of which started in the telephone answering service industry, training did in fact greatly improve and compensation had vastly increased. Thus the findings of the survey are correct. Conversely, the perspective of the authors of the call center literature was wholly in the call center arena. Their assessment of a need for improvement was likewise consistent with that point of view. As such, those in the telephone answering service industry who are becoming call centers did greatly improve training and had less cause for concern about compensation issues, but they cannot rest on their past accomplishments and need to further enhance their processes and make ongoing improvements. Thus, TSR training and compensation will be viewed as key issues in becoming a call center.

Recommendations

Now that the survey results have been summarized and integrated with the findings of the literature search, a composite picture can be painted. This portrait will present the recommended course of action to allow a telephone answering service to become a call center.

First, there were the essential elements which should be present. If these are absent or inadequate, the telephone answering service must first address and correct them. These essentials are to be able to find, train, and adequately compensate TSRs, determine the right technology, retain their sales staff, effectively sell their service, and be committed to growth through sales and marketing.

Five universal truths were discovered which suggest concerns to be addressed, while not essential to success, they are nonetheless dilemmas to tackle. These issues were to increase TSR retention, hire sales staff effectively, increase technological competence, acquire needed technology, and understand and follow governmental regulations.

Areas of focus were also advanced. The first was to maintain attention to TSR issues by lengthening training time, increasing training dollars and staffing budgets, coaching, improving retention, enhancing compensation, and implementing telecommuting. Second, was to maintain sales and marketing expertise, using it to achieve growth. Lastly, was to pursue and implement key technologies, such as computer-telephony integration, interactive voice response, automatic call distribution, skills-based routing, and workforce management software, along with becoming web-enabled, offering telecommuting, and going virtual.

Finally, it is warranted to be cognizant of and prepare for significant call center characteristics. These were longer call durations, extensive use of toll-free numbers, technological intensity, higher occupancy rates, and multiple locations. Then highlight competitive advantages such as 24 x 7 operation and superior service levels.

Conclusion

The purpose of this endeavor was to determine a process by which a telephone answering service could become a call center; this was accomplished and documented. Along the way, however, the exciting reality and bright future of the call center industry was discovered. Most importantly, however, it was verified that there is financial justification and rewards to pursue this path. All that is left undone is to implement the steps contained herein and to move forward.

APPENDIX A: TAS INDUSTRY STRENGTHS

Table 27: <u>Summary of Strengths</u>

Category	Number of Answers	Percent of Participants	Percent of Total Answers
Flexibility	14	50%	20%
Staff ("Live" service)	13	46%	19%
Technology	11	39%	16%
Customer Focused	7	25%	10%
24 x 7	5	18%	7%
Established business	3	11%	4%
Multiple niches to serve	2	7%	3%
Solution oriented	2	7%	3%
Can manage entry-level staff	2	7%	3%
<u>Other</u>	<u>11</u>	<u>na</u>	<u>16%</u>
Total	70	na	100% *

* Adjusted for rounding

(DeHaan, 1998, p. 122)

APPENDIX B: TAS INDUSTRY WEAKNESSES

Table 28: Summary of Weaknesses

Category	Number of Answers	Percent of Participants	Percent of Total Answers
Low rates	11	39%	14%
Poor management skills	10	36%	13%
Poor marketing ability	9	32%	11%
Poor service	8	29%	10%
Technology	6	21%	8%
Low pay (wages)	5	18%	6%
Bad image	5	18%	6%
Entry-level employees	5	18%	6%
Competition from technology	4	14%	5%
Under capitalization	4	14%	5%
Labor intensive	4	14%	5%
Inadequate training	2	7%	3%

Other	6	na	8%
Total	70	na	100% *

* Adjusted for rounding

(DeHaan, 1998, p. 125)

APPENDIX C: TAS INDUSTRY OPPORTUNITIES

Table 29: Summary of Opportunities

. Category	Number of Answers	Percent of Participants
Technology	13	15%
Telephone order-taking	9	11%
Internet	6	7%
Niche markets	6	7%
One-stop shopping	5	6%
Geographic expansion	4	5%
Help desk service	4	5%
Consolidation	3	4%
Customer service lines	3	4%
Marketing	2	2%
Enhanced services	2	2%
Outsourcing	2	2%

Overflow calls	2	2%
Integration with voice mail	2	2%
"Live" service	2	2%
Other	20	24%
Total	85	100% *

* Adjusted for rounding

(DeHaan, 1998, p. 130)

APPENDIX D: INDUSTRY THREATS

Table 30: <u>Summary of Threats</u>

Category	Number of Answers	Percent of Participants
Competitive forces	11	15%
Labor pressures	8	11%
Automation	5	7%
Technology	5	7%
Unprofessional	5	7%
Complacent	4	5%
Call centers	3	4%
Negative public perception	3	4%
Undercapitalization	3	4%
Low pricing	3	4%
Weak management	3	4%
Other answering services	2	3%

Bad debt	2	3%
Decreased demand for service	2	3%
Lack of vision for the future	2	3%
<u>Other</u>	<u>13</u>	<u>17%</u>
Totals	24	100% *

* Adjusted for rounding

(DeHaan, 1998, p. 137)

Appendix E: TAS Recommendations

The basic six

- Strive for flexibility

- Continue to be customer focused

- Improve management skills

- Enhance service

- Enlighten staffing

- Increase employment attractiveness

The foundation

- Perform a SWOT analysis

- Develop a strategic plan

The near universal

- Increase rates

- Improve sales and marketing efforts

- Capitalize on twenty-four-hour staffing

Major recommendations

- Diversify into telephone order-taking

- Pursue internet opportunities

- Invest in technology

Alternate parallel recommendation

- Growth via acquisition

Figure 22. Recommendations to Prepare for the Future.

(DeHaan, 1998, p. 168).

APPENDIX F: TWELVE TYPICAL CAUSES OF TSR TURNOVER

1. The pace of the work.

2. Feeling a lack of control or powerlessness.

3. Repetitious work.

4. Frustration over not being able to perform job as desired.

5. Being restricted to one's desk (being confined).

6. Working in a strictly controlled environment.

7. The feeling or perception of being too closely monitored.

8. Feeling unappreciated.

9. The need to continually handle complaints and problems.

10. Working non-traditional hours (weekends, nights, holidays).

11. Low pay or inadequate compensation package.

12. Better opportunities at other companies or other positions.

Figure 23. Twelve Typical Causes of TSR Turnover

(QueueTips, 1999a).

Appendix G: Ten Call Center Trends

1. Personalized delivery of electronic services

2. Mass delivery of electronic services

3. Increased support efficiencies

4. Bigger workload

5. More services will be outsourced

6. More virtual call centers

7. Globalization

8. Continued merger mania

9. Evolving profiles of customers

10. More time and performance demands on staff

Figure 24. Ten Call Center Trends

(Rose, 1998).

Appendix H: Email Solicitation for Survey Participation

Subject: Request for participation in Industry survey

Date: Mon, 8 Nov 1999

From: Peter L. DeHaan

To: _____

[This email was sent to four email lists; therefore, you may have gotten more than one copy.]

Hello,

I invite you to participate in a survey to measure past changes and project future trends within the industry.

This survey is being conducted in connection with research for my Ph.D. dissertation, measuring the changing dynamics in the TeleServices/Call Center industry. All individual responses will remain confidential; only aggregate data will be shared and included in my dissertation.

The **survey** is designed to be easy to complete and should take less than five minutes. To participate, **call 616-553-xxxx from a fax machine** or

send an email request to dehaan@xxxxxxx.net; put "survey" in the subject line.

- Each participant will receive the compiled results of the survey.

- *__Each industry group__, which has a measurable response, will receive a __private summation of their members' surveys__, contrasted to the industry as a whole.*

Please take a few moments to obtain and complete the survey so that you and your association can benefit from the results. **We need a good response from each organization's members to be able to provide specific analysis for the group.**

Thank you.

--

Peter DeHaan

Figure 25. Mail List Email to Solicit Survey Participation

Appendix I: User Groups and Associations

By email:

Axon User Group CAM-X

CEO

NAEO

SNUG

WSTA

By fax:

ACETS

ASTAA

ATA

GLTSA

SATAS

By email & fax:

ATSI

NEAT

PIN

TUG

TUNe:

By letter:

BCSI

Figure 26. User Group Contact List.

Appendix J: Example of Email to Industry Groups

Subject: Request for participation in Industry survey

Date: Mon, 8 Nov 1999

From: Peter L. DeHaan

To: _____

I invite your association's members to participate in a trade survey to measure past changes and project future trends within the industry.

This survey is being conducted in connection with research for my Ph.D. dissertation, measuring the changing dynamics in the TeleServices/Call Center industry. All individual responses will remain confidential; only aggregate data will be shared and included in my dissertation.

The survey is designed to be easy to complete and should take less than five minutes. To participate, your members can call 616-553-xxxx from a fax machine or send an email request to dehaan@xxxxxxx.net; put "survey" in the subject line.

· Each participant will receive the compiled results of the survey.

· Each industry group, which has a measurable response, will receive a private summation of their members' surveys, contrasted to the industry as a whole.

Please share this opportunity with your members and encourage them to participate. We need a good response from your members to be able to provide you with a specific analysis of your organization.

If you have any questions about this, please call me.

Thank you.

--

Peter L DeHaan

Figure 27. Example of Email to Industry Groups.

Appendix K: Example of Fax and Letter to Industry Groups

ATA

Fax: 818-766-xxxx

I invite ATA members to participate in a trade survey to measure past changes and project future trends within the industry.

This survey is being conducted in connection with research for my Ph.D. dissertation, measuring the changing dynamics in the TeleServices/Call Center industry. All individual responses will remain confidential; only aggregate data will be shared and included in my dissertation.

The **survey** is designed to be easy to complete and should take less than five minutes. To participate, your members can **call 616-553-xxxx from a fax machine** or **send an email request to dehaan@xxxxxxx.net;** put "survey" in the subject line.

- Each participant will receive the compiled results of the survey.

- *Each industry group, which has a measurable response, will receive a private summation of their members' surveys, contrasted to the industry as a whole.*

Please share this opportunity with your members and encourage them to participate. **We need a good response from your members to be able to provide you with a specific analysis of your organization.**

If you have any questions about this, please call me.

Thank you,

Peter L. DeHaan

Figure 28. Example of Fax and Letter to Industry Groups.

Appendix L: TeleServices/Call Center Survey

This survey examines changing conditions in the TeleServices/Call Center Industry and will be used as research for my Ph.D. dissertation. All responses will be kept confidential. Participants are eligible to receive the compiled survey results.

Thank you for your assistance with this research.

A Look at the Past

1. Approximately what year was your organization or division founded?
_____

2. When ***first started***, it was viewed primarily as *(check only one):*

___ A Telephone Answering Service

___ A TeleServices company

___ A Call Center

3. When ***first started,*** which of the following were ***major*** concerns? *(select all that apply)*

Operator/TSR (Telephone Service Representative) Issues

___ Finding TSRs to hire

__ Training TSRs

__ Keeping TSRs

__ Providing adequate TSR compensation

__ Scheduling TSRs

__ Dealing with TSR staffing issues

Sales & Marketing Issues

__ Hiring good sales staff

__ Training sales staff

__ Keeping sales staff

__ Providing adequate sales representative compensation

__ Finding effective marketing promotions

__ Affording marketing promotions

Technical Issues

__ Understanding technology

__ Finding the right technology

__ Affording the right technology

__ Installing and maintaining equipment

Financial Issues

__ Keeping financial records

__ Complying with government reports and forms

__ Obtaining financing

4. On the previous question (question 3), circle the ***most*** important concern.

A View of the Present

5. Over the ***past few years*** your number of accounts has *(check only one)*:

__ Increased greatly

__ Increased somewhat

__ Stayed the same

__ Decreased slightly

__ Decreased greatly

6. Over the ***past few years*** your revenue has *(check only one)*:

__ Increased greatly

__ Increased somewhat

__ Stayed the same

__ Decreased slightly

__ Decreased greatly

7. Over the ***past few years*** your number of calls has *(check only one)*:

__ Increased greatly

__ Increased somewhat

__ Stayed the same

__ Decreased slightly

__ Decreased greatly

8. Over the *past few years* your time per call has *(check only one)*:

__ Increased greatly

__ Increased somewhat

__ Stayed the same

__ Decreased slightly

__ Decreased greatly

9. At *present* which of the following *best* describes your organization/division *(check only one)*

__ A Telephone Answering Service

__ A TeleServices company

__ A Call Center

10. At *present* which of the following are *major* concerns? *(select all that apply)*

Operator/TSR (Telephone Service Representative) Issues

__ Finding TSRs to hire

__ Training TSRs

___ Keeping TSRs

___ Providing adequate TSR compensation

___ Scheduling TSRs

___ Dealing with TSR staffing issues

Sales & Marketing Issues

___ Hiring good sales staff

___ Training sales staff

___ Keeping sales staff

___ Providing adequate sales representative compensation

___ Finding effective marketing promotions

___ Affording marketing promotions

Technical Issues

___ Understanding technology

___ Finding the right technology

___ Affording the right technology

___ Installing and maintaining equipment

Financial Issues

___ Keeping financial records

___ Complying with government reports and forms

___ Obtaining financing

11. On the previous question (question 10), circle the **most** important concern.

Plans for the Future

12. In the **future** do you want your organization/division to be primarily (check only one):

___ A Telephone Answering Service

___ A TeleServices company

___ A Call Center

13. When looking at the **future**, which of the following do you think will be major concerns? (select all that apply)

Operator/TSR (Telephone Service Representative) Issues

___ Finding TSRs to hire

___ Training TSRs

___ Keeping TSRs

___ Providing adequate TSR compensation

___ Scheduling TSRs

___ Dealing with TSR staffing issues

Sales & Marketing Issues

___ Hiring good sales staff

___ Training sales staff

___ Keeping sales staff

___ Providing adequate sales representative compensation

___ Finding effective marketing promotions

___ Affording marketing promotions

Technical Issues

___ Understanding technology

___ Finding the right technology

___ Affording the right technology

___ Installing and maintaining equipment

Financial Issues

___ Keeping financial records

___ Complying with government reports and forms

___ Obtaining financing

14. On the previous question (question 13), circle the ***most*** important concern.

15. In the ***future***, what is the overall direction for your organization/division?

___ Scale back (to become more manageable, less stressful, or more profitable, etc.).

__ Position it to be sold.

__ Maintain things as is.

__ Seek to grow through acquisitions.

__ Seek to grow through sales and marketing.

16. In the previous question (question 15) circle the *most* likely or desired direction.

Profile Information

17. Your title/position: _____

18. Your length of time in the industry: _____

19. If you are a member of an industry association which is interested in a group profile, please list the association(s) (optional):

_____

20. If you wish to receive the survey results, please include your email address (optional):

_____ @ _____

Thank you for being part of this research.

Your time and input is greatly appreciated.

Please fax the completed survey to **616-553-xxxx.**

APPENDIX M: KEY SURVEY DATES

Table 31: Chronological Listing of Key Survey Activities

Activity	Date
Email survey solicitation sent:	November 8,1999
First request for participation received:	November 8, 1999
Follow up letter to industry groups sent:	November 9 – 12, 1999
First survey sent out via email:	November 9, 1999
First completed survey returned:	November 10, 1999
Last request for participation received:	December 3, 1999
Last survey form sent out via email:	December 4, 1999
Last completed survey returned:	December 10, 1999

APPENDIX N: RESPONSES BY INDUSTRY GROUP

Table 32: Responses by Industry Group

Group	# of Surveys	% of Surveys
ATSI	16	36%
NAEO	15	34%
CAM-X	9	20%
PIN	5	11%
CEO	4	9%
SNUG	3	7%
IVMA	2	5%
ASTAA	1	2%
GLTSA	1	2%
WSTA	1	2%
TUNe	1	2%
ACETS	0	0%

ATA	0	0%
Axon User Group	0	0%
BCSI	0	0%
NEAT	0	0%
SATAS	0	0%
TUG	0	0%

APPENDIX O: SURVEY RESULTS

Computer output from the survey analyses is included in the next three Appendices. Appendix O is the overall results of all surveys; Appendix P is the two survey subsets (future call centers and existing call centers, both contrasted to the remaining surveys); and Appendix Q is the results for three industry groups (ATSI, NAEO, and CAM-X).

The output does not present the information in the same order as the survey but was rearranged so as to allow comparisons and trends to be easily determined and presented within a minimal amount of space. As such some explanation is in order.

Each analysis takes two pages; the most important data (concerns) is presented on the first page.

The first column of the output shows the survey questions which are being addressed. The second column includes a brief description of the question or topic. All results are displayed to the left of these descriptions. Related answers have been grouped together, such as past, present, and future responses.

On the first page, the results from the past, present, and future are shown side by side. Each of these three time frames is analyzed three ways. The first, "percent of all," gives the percentage of respondents who picked that answer. The second, "group percentage," reports the percent of responses for that particular group of concerns (that is, for TSR, sales, technical, or financial). The third, "percent of sub-group," gives the relative percent of responses within that particular group.

On the second page, both the number of responses and their percentage of the total are included for each item. Lastly, on the lower right corner, there is a trend analysis for questions two, nine, and twelve. This shows the migration of the participants' organizations between telephone answering service (TAS), teleservice (TS), and call center (CC) activity.

This same format is used for the following two appendices as well.

Survey Results

All Responses

ALL RESPONSES

3,10,13 All Concerns:

	Past % of All	Past Group %	Past % Sub Group	Present % of All	Present Group %	Present % Sub Group	Future % of All	Future Group %	Future % Sub Group
TSR		33%			41%			38%	
Finding TSRs	5%		18%	8%		20%	8%		22%
Training TSRs	7%		23%	5%		13%	4%		11%
Keeping TSRs	6%		21%	9%		21%	8%		21%
Providing Compensation	4%		13%	5%		13%	6%		17%
Scheduling TSRs	3%		11%	6%		14%	4%		11%
Dealing w/ Staffing issues	4%		13%	7%		17%	7%		18%
Sales		26%			28%			29%	
Hiring	5%		21%	8%		28%	9%		30%
Training	3%		12%	4%		16%	3%		12%
Keeping	1%		6%	3%		10%	4%		13%
Providing Compensation	1%		6%	3%		12%	3%		11%
Finding effective marketing	6%		26%	7%		24%	6%		20%
Affording marketing	7%		29%	3%		11%	4%		15%
Technical		24%			22%			23%	
Understanding	6%		27%	6%		26%	6%		25%
Finding technology	5%		25%	4%		20%	5%		24%
Affording	5%		25%	7%		30%	7%		32%
Installing/maintain	5%		23%	5%		25%	4%		19%
Financial		17%			10%			10%	
Keeping records	5%		30%	2%		22%	1%		14%
Complying	5%		30%	4%		44%	4%		43%
Obtaining financing	6%		40%	3%		33%	4%		43%

4,11,14 Most important concern:

	Past % of All	Past Group %	Past % Sub Group	Present % of All	Present Group %	Present % Sub Group	Future % of All	Future Group %	Future % Sub Group
TSR		34%			51%			40%	
Finding TSRs	7%		21%	19%		38%	11%		28%
Training TSRs	5%		14%	8%		16%	8%		19%
Keeping TSRs	8%		23%	11%		22%	14%		34%
Providing Compensation	8%		24%	3%		6%	3%		6%
Scheduling TSRs	2%		6%	6%		11%	3%		6%
Dealing w/ Staffing issues	4%		12%	3%		6%	3%		6%
Sales		31%			21%			12%	
Hiring	7%		22%	8%		39%	10%		79%
Training	4%		13%	3%		13%	0%		0%
Keeping	1%		4%	0%		2%	0%		0%
Providing Compensation	1%		4%	0%		2%	0%		0%
Finding effective marketing	8%		24%	9%		42%	3%		21%
Affording marketing	10%		32%	0%		2%	0%		0%
Technical		4%			19%			32%	
Understanding	1%		32%	7%		39%	14%		44%
Finding technology	1%		16%	6%		32%	9%		30%
Affording	2%		37%	3%		16%	4%		14%
Installing/maintain	1%		16%	2%		13%	4%		12%
Financial		30%			9%			16%	
Keeping records	6%		21%	2%		27%	3%		21%
Complying	4%		12%	4%		40%	8%		53%
Obtaining financing	20%		67%	3%		33%	4%		26%

Survey Results

All Responses (continued)

ALL RESPONSES

		Low	High	Ave
1	Year founded:	1931	1992	1970
	Year founded/bought/started:	1931	1998	1976
18	Time in the industry:	2	40	16

		Past		Present		Future	
		%	Count	%	Count	%	Count
2,9,12	Organization viewed as:						
	Telephone Answering Svc	93%	42	29%	13	16%	7
	TeleServices company	4%	2	42%	19	38%	17
	Call Center	2%	1	29%	13	47%	21
			45		45		45

		Number of Accounts	Revenue	Number of Calls	Length of Calls
5,6,7,8	The following items:				
	Increased greatly	36%	42%	38%	20%
	Increased somewhat	32%	42%	33%	36%
	Stayed the same	11%	7%	16%	29%
	Decreased slightly	14%	4%	7%	16%
	Decreased greatly	7%	4%	7%	0%
		100%	100%	100%	100%

		All Answers		Most Likely	
15,16	In the future you plan to:				
	Scale back	7%	5	10%	4
	Position it to be sold	12%	9	5%	2
	Maintain business as is	5%	4	10%	4
	Pursue acquisitions	26%	19	17%	7
	Increase sales & marketing	49%	36	59%	24
			73		41

17	Title/position:		
	Pres, CEO, Owner	76%	34
	Op Mgr, VP Op, Dir Op, GM	22%	10
	Sales Mgr	2%	1
			45

19	Association memberships (44 responded):		
	ATSI	36%	16
	NAEO	34%	15
	CAM-X	20%	9
	PIN	11%	5
	CEO	9%	4
	SNUG	7%	3
	IVMA	5%	2
	ASTAA	2%	1
	GLTSA	2%	1
	TUNe	2%	1
	WSTA	2%	1

20	Wants To Receive Results:	98%	44

Trend Analysis - Breakdown:		
Past / Present / Future		
TAS / TAS / TAS	11%	5
TAS / TAS / TS	11%	5
TAS / TAS / CC	4%	2
TAS / TS / TAS	2%	1
TAS / TS / TS	27%	12
TAS / TS / CC	11%	5
TAS / CC / CC	27%	12
TS / TAS / TAS	2%	1
TS / TAS / CC	2%	1
CC / CC / CC	2%	1
		45

Trend Analysis - Summary:		
Stay the Same	13%	6
Have Changed	53%	24
Will Change	18%	8
Ongoing Change	11%	5
Switch Back to TAS	4%	2
		45

APPENDIX P: RESULTS FOR SUBSETS

Results for Subsets

Future Call Centers

Future Call Centers	Past % of All	Group %	% Sub Group	Present % of All	Group %	% Sub Group	Future % of All	Group %	% Sub Group
3,10,13 All Concerns:									
TSR		37%			40%			36%	
Finding TSRs	5%		15%	7%		18%	8%		22%
Training TSRs	8%		26%	4%		10%	3%		8%
Keeping TSRs	7%		23%	9%		24%	8%		22%
Providing Compensation	5%		15%	7%		17%	7%		19%
Scheduling TSRs	2%		8%	7%		17%	5%		13%
Dealing w/ Staffing issues	4%		13%	6%		15%	6%		16%
Sales		25%			25%			28%	
Hiring	5%		22%	8%		31%	9%		31%
Training	2%		8%	3%		13%	3%		10%
Keeping	2%		8%	3%		13%	4%		15%
Providing Compensation	1%		3%	3%		11%	2%		8%
Finding effective marketing	6%		28%	5%		20%	6%		21%
Affording marketing	7%		31%	3%		11%	4%		15%
Technical		22%			25%			27%	
Understanding	4%		22%	6%		24%	5%		20%
Finding technology	5%		28%	5%		20%	8%		28%
Affording	4%		22%	8%		31%	8%		30%
Installing/maintain	5%		28%	6%		24%	6%		22%
Financial		17%			9%			9%	
Keeping records	4%		25%	3%		29%	2%		19%
Complying	4%		29%	4%		41%	3%		38%
Obtaining financing	7%		46%	3%		29%	4%		44%
4,11,14 Most important concern:									
TSR		37%			51%			38%	
Finding TSRs	10%		27%	11%		22%	4%		11%
Training TSRs	4%		11%	6%		11%	4%		11%
Keeping TSRs	6%		15%	18%		36%	16%		43%
Providing Compensation	10%		27%	6%		11%	4%		11%
Scheduling TSRs	4%		11%	6%		11%	4%		11%
Dealing w/ Staffing issues	3%		8%	6%		11%	4%		11%
Sales		25%			13%			12%	
Hiring	7%		27%	8%		63%	12%		100%
Training	1%		4%	1%		7%	0%		0%
Keeping	1%		4%	1%		7%	0%		0%
Providing Compensation	1%		4%	1%		7%	0%		0%
Finding effective marketing	1%		4%	1%		7%	0%		0%
Affording marketing	14%		57%	1%		7%	0%		0%
Technical		7%			24%			22%	
Understanding	3%		40%	11%		47%	12%		53%
Finding technology	1%		20%	6%		24%	1%		6%
Affording	1%		20%	7%		29%	8%		35%
Installing/maintain	1%		20%	0%		0%	1%		6%
Financial		31%			13%			28%	
Keeping records	6%		19%	6%		44%	7%		25%
Complying	0%		0%	6%		44%	12%		44%
Obtaining financing	26%		81%	1%		11%	8%		30%

Results for Subsets

Future Call Centers (continued)

Future Call Centers

	Low	High	Ave
1 Year founded:	1945	1992	1974
Year founded/bought/started:	1951	1992	1978
18 Time in the industry:	3	30	16

	Past		Present		Future	
2,9,12 Organization viewed as:	%	Count	%	Count	%	Count
Telephone Answering Svc	90%	19	14%	3	0%	0
TeleServices company	5%	1	24%	5	0%	0
Call Center	5%	1	62%	13	100%	21
		21		21		21

	Number of Accounts	Revenue	Number of Calls	Length of Calls
5,6,7,8 The following items:				
Increased greatly	29%	38%	38%	29%
Increased somewhat	38%	52%	33%	43%
Stayed the same	14%	5%	14%	19%
Decreased slightly	19%	5%	10%	10%
Decreased greatly	0%	0%	5%	0%
	100%	100%	100%	100%

	All Answers		Most Likely	
15,16 In the future you plan to:				
Scale back	9%	3	11%	2
Position it to be sold	14%	5	0%	0
Maintain business as is	3%	1	6%	1
Pursue acquisitions	23%	8	11%	2
Increase sales & marketing	51%	18	72%	13
		35		18

17 Title/position:		
Pres, CEO, Owner	81%	17
Op Mgr, VP Op, Dir Op, GM	14%	3
Sales Mgr	5%	1
		21

Trend Analysis - Breakdown:		
Past / Present / Future		
TAS / TAS / TAS	0%	0
TAS / TAS / TS	0%	0
TAS / TAS / CC	10%	2
TAS / TS / TAS	0%	0
TAS / TS / TS	0%	0
TAS / TS / CC	24%	5
TAS / CC / CC	57%	12
TS / TAS / TAS	0%	0
TS / TAS / CC	5%	1
CC / CC / CC	5%	1
		21

19 Association memberships (44 responded):		
ATSI	25%	5
NAEO	40%	8
CAM-X	15%	3
PIN	10%	2
CEO	10%	2
SNUG	0%	0
IVMA	0%	0
ASTAA	5%	1
GLTSA	5%	1
TUNe	5%	1
WSTA	5%	1

Trend Analysis - Summary:		
Stay the Same	5%	1
Have Changed	57%	12
Will Change	14%	3
Ongoing Change	24%	5
Switch Back to TAS	0%	0
		21

20 Wants To Receive Results:	95%	20

Results for Subsets

Those Who Will Not Become a Call Center

Not Future Call Centers	Past % of All	Group %	% Sub Group	Present % of All	Group %	% Sub Group	Future % of All	Group %	% Sub Group
3,10,13 All Concerns:									
TSR		29%			41%			39%	
Finding TSRs	5%		22%	9%		22%	9%		22%
Training TSRs	5%		20%	7%		17%	5%		13%
Keeping TSRs	5%		20%	8%		19%	8%		19%
Providing Compensation	3%		11%	4%		10%	6%		15%
Scheduling TSRs	4%		15%	5%		12%	4%		10%
Dealing w/ Staffing issues	3%		13%	8%		19%	8%		21%
Sales		27%			30%			31%	
Hiring	4%		19%	7%		25%	9%		28%
Training	3%		14%	5%		18%	4%		13%
Keeping	1%		5%	2%		7%	3%		11%
Providing Compensation	2%		10%	4%		13%	4%		13%
Finding effective marketing	5%		24%	8%		27%	6%		19%
Affording marketing	7%		29%	3%		11%	5%		15%
Technical		26%			19%			19%	
Understanding	7%		32%	5%		28%	6%		33%
Finding technology	5%		22%	4%		19%	3%		18%
Affording	6%		27%	5%		28%	6%		33%
Installing/maintain	4%		20%	5%		25%	3%		15%
Financial		18%			10%			11%	
Keeping records	5%		34%	2%		16%	1%		11%
Complying	5%		31%	5%		47%	5%		47%
Obtaining financing	5%		34%	4%		37%	5%		42%
4,11,14 Most important concern:									
TSR		32%			50%			43%	
Finding TSRs	5%		16%	25%		51%	18%		42%
Training TSRs	5%		16%	10%		20%	11%		25%
Keeping TSRs	10%		32%	6%		12%	12%		27%
Providing Compensation	7%		21%	1%		3%	1%		2%
Scheduling TSRs	0%		0%	6%		12%	1%		2%
Dealing w/ Staffing issues	5%		16%	1%		3%	1%		2%
Sales		37%			28%			12%	
Hiring	7%		18%	9%		31%	7%		60%
Training	7%		18%	4%		15%	0%		0%
Keeping	2%		5%	0%		0%	0%		0%
Providing Compensation	2%		5%	0%		0%	0%		0%
Finding effective marketing	13%		36%	15%		54%	5%		40%
Affording marketing	7%		18%	0%		0%	0%		0%
Technical		2%			15%			40%	
Understanding	0%		0%	4%		29%	16%		40%
Finding technology	0%		0%	7%		43%	17%		42%
Affording	2%		100%	0%		0%	1%		3%
Installing/maintain	0%		0%	4%		29%	6%		15%
Financial		30%			7%			5%	
Keeping records	7%		22%	0%		0%	0%		0%
Complying	7%		22%	2%		33%	5%		100%
Obtaining financing	17%		56%	4%		67%	0%		0%

Results for Subsets

Those Who Will Not Become a Call Center (continued)

Not Future Call Centers

		Low	High	Ave
1	Year founded:	1931	1989	1967
	Year founded/bought/started:	1931	1998	1974
18	Time in the industry:	2	40	16

		Past		Present		Future	
		%	Count	%	Count	%	Count
2,9,12	Organization viewed as:						
	Telephone Answering Svc	96%	23	42%	10	29%	7
	TeleServices company	4%	1	58%	14	71%	17
	Call Center	0%	0	0%	0	0%	0
			24		24		24

		Number of Accounts	Revenue	Number of Calls	Length of Calls
5,6,7,8	The following items:				
	Increased greatly	43%	46%	38%	13%
	Increased somewhat	26%	33%	33%	29%
	Stayed the same	9%	8%	17%	38%
	Decreased slightly	9%	4%	4%	21%
	Decreased greatly	13%	8%	8%	0%
		100%	100%	100%	100%

		All Answers		Most Likely	
15,16	In the future you plan to:				
	Scale back	5%	2	9%	2
	Position it to be sold	11%	4	9%	2
	Maintain business as is	8%	3	13%	3
	Pursue acquisitions	29%	11	22%	5
	Increase sales & marketing	47%	18	48%	11
			38		23

				Trend Analysis - Breakdown:		
17	Title/position:			Past / Present / Future		
	Pres, CEO, Owner	71%	17	TAS / TAS / TAS	21%	5
	Op Mgr, VP Op, Dir Op, GM	29%	7	TAS / TAS / TS	21%	5
	Sales Mgr	0%	0	TAS / TAS / CC	0%	0
			24	TAS / TS / TAS	4%	1
				TAS / TS / TS	50%	12
19	Association memberships (44 responded):			TAS / TS / CC	0%	0
	ATSI	46%	11	TAS / CC / CC	0%	0
	NAEO	29%	7	TS / TAS / TAS	4%	1
	CAM-X	25%	6	TS / TAS / CC	0%	0
	PIN	13%	3	CC / CC / CC	0%	0
	CEO	8%	2			24
	SNUG	13%	3			
	IVMA	8%	2	Trend Analysis - Summary:		
	ASTAA	0%	0	Stay the Same	21%	5
	GLTSA	0%	0	Have Changed	50%	12
	TUNe	0%	0	Will Change	21%	5
	WSTA	0%	0	Ongoing Change	0%	0
				Switch Back to TAS	8%	2
20	Wants To Receive Results:	100%	24			24

Results for Subsets

Existing Call Centers

Existing Call Centers	Past % of All	Past Group %	Past % Sub Group	Present % of All	Present Group %	Present % Sub Group	Future % of All	Future Group %	Future % Sub Group
3,10,13 All Concerns:									
TSR		33%			43%			38%	
Finding TSRs	4%		15%	7%		17%	8%		20%
Training TSRs	7%		26%	5%		13%	4%		10%
Keeping TSRs	6%		22%	10%		23%	8%		20%
Providing Compensation	3%		11%	7%		17%	7%		18%
Scheduling TSRs	2%		7%	7%		17%	6%		15%
Dealing w/ Staffing issues	5%		19%	5%		13%	7%		18%
Sales		22%			22%			25%	
Hiring	5%		28%	7%		33%	10%		38%
Training	3%		17%	3%		13%	4%		15%
Keeping	1%		6%	3%		13%	2%		8%
Providing Compensation	0%		0%	2%		8%	1%		4%
Finding effective marketing	4%		22%	5%		21%	4%		15%
Affording marketing	5%		28%	3%		13%	5%		19%
Technical		27%			26%			28%	
Understanding	5%		23%	5%		17%	4%		14%
Finding technology	6%		27%	6%		24%	9%		31%
Affording	5%		23%	9%		34%	9%		31%
Installing/maintain	6%		27%	6%		24%	7%		24%
Financial		18%			9%			10%	
Keeping records	3%		20%	2%		20%	1%		10%
Complying	4%		27%	4%		40%	4%		40%
Obtaining financing	8%		53%	4%		40%	5%		50%
4,11,14 Most important concern:									
TSR		39%			60%			44%	
Finding TSRs	14%		35%	15%		25%	6%		13%
Training TSRs	5%		12%	7%		11%	6%		13%
Keeping TSRs	7%		18%	17%		29%	16%		37%
Providing Compensation	5%		12%	7%		11%	6%		13%
Scheduling TSRs	5%		12%	7%		11%	6%		13%
Dealing w/ Staffing issues	5%		12%	7%		11%	6%		13%
Sales		30%			19%			10%	
Hiring	9%		31%	12%		63%	10%		100%
Training	0%		0%	1%		7%	0%		0%
Keeping	0%		0%	1%		7%	0%		0%
Providing Compensation	0%		0%	1%		7%	0%		0%
Finding effective marketing	0%		0%	1%		7%	0%		0%
Affording marketing	20%		69%	1%		7%	0%		0%
Technical		11%			19%			27%	
Understanding	5%		40%	8%		44%	10%		38%
Finding technology	2%		20%	0%		0%	2%		8%
Affording	2%		20%	10%		56%	13%		46%
Installing/maintain	2%		20%	0%		0%	2%		8%
Financial		20%			2%			19%	
Keeping records	0%		0%	0%		0%	3%		15%
Complying	0%		0%	0%		0%	11%		58%
Obtaining financing	20%		100%	2%		100%	5%		26%

Results for Subsets

Existing Call Centers (continued)

Existing Call Centers

		Low	High	Ave
1	Year founded:	1945	1991	1974
	Year founded/bought/started:	1961	1991	1979
18	Time in the industry:	3	28	15

		Past		Present		Future	
		%	Count	%	Count	%	Count
2,9,12	Organization viewed as:						
	Telephone Answering Svc	92%	12	0%	0	0%	0
	TeleServices company	0%	0	0%	0	0%	0
	Call Center	8%	1	100%	13	100%	13
			13		13		13

		Number of Accounts	Revenue	Number of Calls	Length of Calls
5,6,7,8	The following items:				
	Increased greatly	23%	31%	23%	38%
	Increased somewhat	46%	62%	54%	38%
	Stayed the same	23%	8%	15%	15%
	Decreased slightly	8%	0%	8%	8%
	Decreased greatly	0%	0%	0%	0%
		100%	100%	100%	100%

		All Answers		Most Likely	
15,16	In the future you plan to:				
	Scale back	0%	0	0%	0
	Position it to be sold	11%	2	0%	0
	Maintain business as is	5%	1	8%	1
	Pursue acquisitions	26%	5	8%	1
	Increase sales & marketing	58%	11	83%	10
			19		12

17	Title/position:				
	Pres, CEO, Owner	77%	10		
	Op Mgr, VP Op, Dir Op, GM	15%	2		
	Sales Mgr	8%	1		
			13		

19 Association memberships (44 responded):		
ATSI	15%	2
NAEO	46%	6
CAM-X	15%	2
PIN	15%	2
CEO	8%	1
SNUG	0%	0
IVMA	0%	0
ASTAA	0%	0
GLTSA	0%	0
TUNe	0%	0
WSTA	0%	0

20 Wants To Receive Results:	100%	13

Trend Analysis - Breakdown:

Past / Present / Future		
TAS / TAS / TAS	0%	0
TAS / TAS / TS	0%	0
TAS / TAS / CC	0%	0
TAS / TS / TAS	0%	0
TAS / TS / TS	0%	0
TAS / TS / CC	0%	0
TAS / CC / CC	92%	12
TS / TAS / TAS	0%	0
TS / TAS / CC	0%	0
CC / CC / CC	8%	1
		13

Trend Analysis - Summary:

Stay the Same	8%	1
Have Changed	92%	12
Will Change	0%	0
Ongoing Change	0%	0
Switch Back to TAS	0%	0
		13

Results for Subsets

Non Call Centers

Non Call Centers	Past			Present			Future		
	% of All	Group %	% Sub Group	% of All	Group %	% Sub Group	% of All	Group %	% Sub Group
3,10,13 All Concerns:									
TSR		33%			40%			38%	
Finding TSRs	6%		19%	9%		22%	9%		23%
Training TSRs	6%		22%	5%		14%	4%		11%
Keeping TSRs	6%		21%	8%		21%	8%		21%
Providing Compensation	4%		14%	5%		12%	6%		16%
Scheduling TSRs	4%		13%	5%		13%	4%		10%
Dealing w/ Staffing issues	3%		11%	8%		20%	7%		19%
Sales		27%			30%			31%	
Hiring	4%		18%	8%		26%	8%		27%
Training	2%		10%	5%		17%	3%		11%
Keeping	2%		7%	3%		9%	5%		15%
Providing Compensation	2%		8%	4%		13%	4%		13%
Finding effective marketing	6%		27%	7%		25%	7%		21%
Affording marketing	7%		30%	3%		10%	4%		13%
Technical		23%			20%			21%	
Understanding	6%		29%	6%		31%	7%		32%
Finding technology	5%		24%	4%		17%	4%		20%
Affording	5%		25%	5%		27%	7%		32%
Installing/maintain	4%		22%	5%		25%	3%		16%
Financial		17%			10%			10%	
Keeping records	5%		34%	2%		23%	2%		16%
Complying	5%		32%	5%		46%	5%		44%
Obtaining financing	5%		34%	3%		31%	4%		40%
4,11,14 Most important concern:									
TSR		32%			47%			39%	
Finding TSRs	5%		14%	21%		44%	14%		36%
Training TSRs	5%		14%	9%		19%	9%		22%
Keeping TSRs	8%		26%	9%		19%	13%		33%
Providing Compensation	10%		30%	2%		4%	1%		3%
Scheduling TSRs	1%		2%	5%		11%	1%		3%
Dealing w/ Staffing issues	4%		12%	2%		4%	1%		3%
Sales		32%			22%			13%	
Hiring	6%		18%	7%		31%	9%		71%
Training	6%		18%	3%		15%	0%		0%
Keeping	2%		6%	0%		0%	0%		0%
Providing Compensation	2%		6%	0%		0%	0%		0%
Finding effective marketing	11%		34%	12%		54%	4%		29%
Affording marketing	6%		18%	0%		0%	0%		0%
Technical		1%			19%			34%	
Understanding	0%		0%	7%		36%	16%		46%
Finding technology	0%		0%	9%		45%	13%		38%
Affording	1%		100%	0%		0%	1%		3%
Installing/maintain	0%		0%	3%		18%	5%		14%
Financial		35%			12%			15%	
Keeping records	9%		26%	3%		29%	4%		25%
Complying	5%		15%	5%		43%	7%		50%
Obtaining financing	21%		59%	3%		29%	4%		25%

Results for Subsets

Non Call Centers (continued)

Non Call Centers

		Low	High	Ave
1	Year founded:	1931	1992	1969
	Year founded/bought/started:	1931	1998	1975
18	Time in the industry:	2	40	16

		Past		Present		Future	
		%	Count	%	Count	%	Count
2,9,12	Organization viewed as:						
	Telephone Answering Svc	94%	30	41%	13	22%	7
	TeleServices company	6%	2	59%	19	53%	17
	Call Center	0%	0	0%	0	25%	8
			32		32		32

		Number of Accounts	Revenue	Number of Calls	Length of Calls
5,6,7,8	The following items:				
	Increased greatly	42%	47%	44%	13%
	Increased somewhat	26%	34%	25%	34%
	Stayed the same	6%	6%	16%	34%
	Decreased slightly	16%	6%	6%	19%
	Decreased greatly	10%	6%	9%	0%
		100%	100%	100%	100%

		All Answers		Most Likely	
15,16	In the future you plan to:				
	Scale back	9%	5	14%	4
	Position it to be sold	13%	7	7%	2
	Maintain business as is	6%	3	10%	3
	Pursue acquisitions	26%	14	21%	6
	Increase sales & marketing	46%	25	48%	14
			54		29

17	Title/position:		
	Pres, CEO, Owner	75%	24
	Op Mgr, VP Op, Dir Op, GM	25%	8
	Sales Mgr	0%	0
			32

19	Association memberships (44 responded):		
	ATSI	45%	14
	NAEO	29%	9
	CAM-X	23%	7
	PIN	10%	3
	CEO	10%	3
	SNUG	10%	3
	IVMA	6%	2
	ASTAA	3%	1
	GLTSA	3%	1
	TUNe	3%	1
	WSTA	3%	1

20	Wants To Receive Results:	97%	31

Trend Analysis - Breakdown:

Past / Present / Future		
TAS / TAS / TAS	16%	5
TAS / TAS / TS	16%	5
TAS / TAS / CC	6%	2
TAS / TS / TAS	3%	1
TAS / TS / TS	38%	12
TAS / TS / CC	16%	5
TAS / CC / CC	0%	0
TS / TAS / TAS	3%	1
TS / TAS / CC	3%	1
CC / CC / CC	0%	0
		32

Trend Analysis - Summary:

Stay the Same	16%	5
Have Changed	38%	12
Will Change	25%	8
Ongoing Change	16%	5
Switch Back to TAS	6%	2
		32

APPENDIX Q: RESULTS FOR INDUSTRY GROUPS

Results for Industry Groups.

ATSI Members

AT SI members	Past			Present			Future		
	% of All	Group %	% Sub Group	% of All	Group %	% Sub Group	% of All	Group %	% Sub Group
3,10,13 All Concerns:									
TSR		34%			44%			42%	
Finding TSRs	4%		14%	10%		23%	11%		26%
Training TSRs	6%		20%	7%		17%	4%		9%
Keeping TSRs	6%		20%	8%		18%	9%		21%
Providing Compensation	5%		17%	6%		13%	6%		13%
Scheduling TSRs	3%		9%	6%		13%	5%		11%
Dealing w/ Staffing issues	6%		20%	7%		15%	8%		19%
Sales		22%			24%			28%	
Hiring	3%		13%	6%		25%	8%		29%
Training	1%		4%	3%		13%	4%		14%
Keeping	1%		4%	1%		6%	4%		14%
Providing Compensation	1%		4%	3%		13%	3%		11%
Finding effective marketing	7%		35%	7%		31%	6%		20%
Affording marketing	8%		39%	3%		13%	3%		11%
Technical		26%			22%			20%	
Understanding	8%		33%	5%		23%	5%		24%
Finding technology	6%		26%	4%		20%	4%		20%
Affording	6%		26%	7%		33%	8%		40%
Installing/maintain	3%		15%	5%		23%	3%		16%
Financial		18%			10%			10%	
Keeping records	6%		37%	2%		23%	2%		17%
Complying	4%		26%	4%		38%	3%		33%
Obtaining financing	6%		37%	4%		38%	5%		50%
4,11,14 Most important concern:									
TSR		26%			63%			65%	
Finding TSRs	1%		5%	32%		51%	22%		33%
Training TSRs	1%		5%	16%		25%	18%		27%
Keeping TSRs	9%		35%	9%		14%	18%		27%
Providing Compensation	4%		15%	2%		4%	3%		4%
Scheduling TSRs	1%		5%	2%		4%	3%		4%
Dealing w/ Staffing issues	9%		35%	2%		4%	3%		4%
Sales		41%			10%			12%	
Hiring	3%		6%	0%		0%	12%		100%
Training	3%		6%	0%		0%	0%		0%
Keeping	3%		6%	0%		0%	0%		0%
Providing Compensation	3%		6%	0%		0%	0%		0%
Finding effective marketing	21%		50%	10%		100%	0%		0%
Affording marketing	10%		25%	0%		0%	0%		0%
Technical		3%			20%			23%	
Understanding	0%		0%	13%		67%	8%		33%
Finding technology	0%		0%	0%		0%	8%		33%
Affording	3%		100%	0%		0%	0%		0%
Installing/maintain	0%		0%	7%		33%	8%		33%
Financial		31%			7%			0%	
Keeping records	8%		25%	0%		0%	0%		0%
Complying	0%		0%	0%		0%	0%		0%
Obtaining financing	23%		75%	7%		100%	0%		0%

Results for Industry Groups.

ATSI Members (continued)

AT SI members

		Low	High	Ave
1	Year founded:	1931	1992	1966
	Year founded/bought/started:	1931	1998	1975
18	Time in the industry:	2	27	16

		Past		Present		Future	
		%	Count	%	Count	%	Count
2,9,12	Organization viewed as:						
	Telephone Answering Svc	100%	16	31%	5	6%	1
	TeleServices company	0%	0	56%	9	63%	10
	Call Center	0%	0	13%	2	31%	5
			16		16		16

		Number of Accounts	Revenue	Number of Calls	Length of Calls
5,6,7,8	The following items:				
	Increased greatly	44%	56%	44%	13%
	Increased somewhat	31%	25%	31%	25%
	Stayed the same	6%	6%	6%	44%
	Decreased slightly	13%	13%	6%	19%
	Decreased greatly	6%	0%	13%	0%
		100%	100%	100%	100%

		All Answers		Most Likely	
15,16	In the future you plan to:				
	Scale back	7%	2	7%	1
	Position it to be sold	15%	4	7%	1
	Maintain business as is	11%	3	20%	3
	Pursue acquisitions	30%	8	20%	3
	Increase sales & marketing	37%	10	47%	7
			27		15

17	Title/position:		
	Pres, CEO, Owner	88%	14
	Op Mgr, VP Op, Dir Op, GM	13%	2
	Sales Mgr	0%	0
			16

19	Association memberships (44 responded):		
	ATSI	100%	16
	NAEO	38%	6
	CAM-X	19%	3
	PIN	25%	4
	CEO	19%	3
	SNUG	19%	3
	IVMA	6%	1
	ASTAA	6%	1
	GLTSA	6%	1
	TUNe	6%	1
	WSTA	6%	1

Trend Analysis - Breakdown:		
Past / Present / Future		
TAS / TAS / TAS	6%	1
TAS / TAS / TS	19%	3
TAS / TAS / CC	13%	2
TAS / TS / TAS	0%	0
TAS / TS / TS	44%	7
TAS / TS / CC	6%	1
TAS / CC / CC	13%	2
TS / TAS / TAS	0%	0
TS / TAS / CC	0%	0
CC / CC / CC	0%	0
		16

Trend Analysis - Summary:		
Stay the Same	6%	1
Have Changed	56%	9
Will Change	31%	5
Ongoing Change	6%	1
Switch Back to TAS	0%	0
		16

20	Wants To Receive Results:	100%	16

Results for Industry Groups.

NAEO Members

NAEO members	Past % of All	Group %	% Sub Group	Present % of All	Group %	% Sub Group	Future % of All	Group %	% Sub Group
3,10,13 All Concerns:									
TSR		35%			38%			38%	
Finding TSRs	5%		15%	8%		20%	8%		22%
Training TSRs	6%		21%	4%		11%	4%		11%
Keeping TSRs	6%		18%	9%		25%	8%		20%
Providing Compensation	5%		15%	5%		14%	6%		16%
Scheduling TSRs	5%		15%	4%		11%	4%		11%
Dealing w/ Staffing issues	5%		18%	7%		18%	8%		20%
Sales		23%			28%			29%	
Hiring	4%		18%	8%		27%	9%		32%
Training	2%		9%	4%		15%	3%		12%
Keeping	1%		5%	3%		9%	4%		15%
Providing Compensation	0%		0%	3%		12%	3%		12%
Finding effective marketing	7%		36%	9%		30%	6%		21%
Affording marketing	6%		32%	2%		6%	3%		9%
Technical		20%			23%			24%	
Understanding	5%		26%	6%		26%	8%		32%
Finding technology	6%		32%	4%		19%	5%		21%
Affording	4%		21%	7%		30%	7%		29%
Installing/maintain	4%		21%	6%		26%	4%		18%
Financial		22%			11%			9%	
Keeping records	6%		33%	2%		15%	0%		0%
Complying	5%		29%	6%		54%	4%		45%
Obtaining financing	7%		38%	3%		31%	5%		55%
4,11,14 Most important concern:									
TSR		47%			44%			29%	
Finding TSRs	11%		24%	21%		46%	5%		18%
Training TSRs	3%		7%	9%		20%	9%		31%
Keeping TSRs	22%		47%	11%		25%	11%		38%
Providing Compensation	6%		13%	1%		3%	1%		4%
Scheduling TSRs	3%		7%	1%		3%	1%		4%
Dealing w/ Staffing issues	1%		3%	1%		3%	1%		4%
Sales		22%			29%			13%	
Hiring	10%		45%	17%		60%	13%		100%
Training	1%		6%	0%		0%	0%		0%
Keeping	1%		6%	0%		0%	0%		0%
Providing Compensation	1%		6%	0%		0%	0%		0%
Finding effective marketing	4%		19%	12%		40%	0%		0%
Affording marketing	3%		16%	0%		0%	0%		0%
Technical		5%			17%			25%	
Understanding	2%		43%	8%		44%	15%		62%
Finding technology	0%		0%	0%		0%	0%		0%
Affording	3%		57%	2%		11%	2%		8%
Installing/maintain	0%		0%	8%		44%	8%		31%
Financial		27%			10%			33%	
Keeping records	8%		31%	0%		0%	0%		0%
Complying	0%		0%	8%		80%	23%		71%
Obtaining financing	19%		69%	2%		20%	10%		29%

Results for Industry Groups.

NAEO Members (continued)

NAEO members

		Low	High	Ave
1	Year founded:	1931	1991	1967
	Year founded/bought/started:	1931	1998	1980
18	Time in the industry:	2	30	14

	Past		Present		Future	
2,9,12 Organization viewed as:	%	Count	%	Count	%	Count
Telephone Answering Svc	93%	14	20%	3	7%	1
TeleServices company	0%	0	40%	6	40%	6
Call Center	7%	1	40%	6	53%	8
		15		15		15

	Number of Accounts	Revenue	Number of Calls	Length of Calls
5,6,7,8 The following items:				
Increased greatly	40%	47%	40%	13%
Increased somewhat	53%	47%	33%	40%
Stayed the same	0%	7%	20%	27%
Decreased slightly	7%	0%	7%	20%
Decreased greatly	0%	0%	0%	0%
	100%	100%	100%	100%

	All Answers		Most Likely	
15,16 In the future you plan to:				
Scale back	8%	2	14%	2
Position it to be sold	16%	4	7%	1
Maintain business as is	4%	1	7%	1
Pursue acquisitions	24%	6	21%	3
Increase sales & marketing	48%	12	50%	7
		25		14

17 Title/position:		
Pres, CEO, Owner	87%	13
Op Mgr, VP Op, Dir Op, GM	7%	1
Sales Mgr	7%	1
		15

Trend Analysis - Breakdown:		
Past / Present / Future		
TAS / TAS / TAS	7%	1
TAS / TAS / TS	13%	2
TAS / TAS / CC	0%	0
TAS / TS / TAS	0%	0
TAS / TS / TS	27%	4
TAS / TS / CC	13%	2
TAS / CC / CC	33%	5
TS / TAS / TAS	0%	0
TS / TAS / CC	0%	0
CC / CC / CC	7%	1
		15

19 Association memberships (44 responded):		
ATSI	40%	6
NAEO	100%	15
CAM-X	13%	2
PIN	0%	0
CEO	7%	1
SNUG	7%	1
IVMA	7%	1
ASTAA	0%	0
GLTSA	0%	0
TUNe	0%	0
WSTA	0%	0

Trend Analysis - Summary:		
Stay the Same	13%	2
Have Changed	60%	9
Will Change	13%	2
Ongoing Change	13%	2
Switch Back to TAS	0%	0
		15

20 Wants To Receive Results:	100%	15

Results for Industry Groups.

CAM-X Members

CAM-X Members	Past			Present			Future		
	% of All	Group %	% Sub Group	% of All	Group %	% Sub Group	% of All	Group %	% Sub Group
3,10,13 All Concerns:									
TSR		34%			42%			37%	
Finding TSRs	5%		17%	7%		16%	7%		20%
Training TSRs	6%		21%	6%		14%	5%		13%
Keeping TSRs	5%		17%	8%		19%	7%		20%
Providing Compensation	4%		13%	8%		19%	6%		17%
Scheduling TSRs	5%		17%	7%		16%	6%		17%
Dealing w/ Staffing issues	5%		17%	7%		16%	5%		13%
Sales		27%			28%			29%	
Hiring	5%		21%	8%		28%	9%		29%
Training	5%		21%	5%		16%	5%		17%
Keeping	0%		0%	3%		12%	4%		13%
Providing Compensation	3%		11%	2%		8%	5%		17%
Finding effective marketing	5%		21%	9%		32%	5%		17%
Affording marketing	6%		26%	1%		4%	2%		8%
Technical		23%			19%			23%	
Understanding	6%		31%	6%		29%	6%		26%
Finding technology	4%		19%	5%		24%	6%		26%
Affording	8%		38%	5%		24%	6%		26%
Installing/maintain	3%		13%	5%		24%	5%		21%
Financial		17%			10%			11%	
Keeping records	5%		33%	3%		33%	2%		22%
Complying	4%		25%	2%		22%	2%		22%
Obtaining financing	6%		42%	5%		44%	6%		56%
4,11,14 Most important concern:									
TSR		18%			32%			21%	
Finding TSRs	0%		0%	14%		44%	0%		0%
Training TSRs	0%		0%	0%		0%	17%		80%
Keeping TSRs	4%		20%	4%		11%	4%		20%
Providing Compensation	14%		80%	0%		0%	0%		0%
Scheduling TSRs	0%		0%	14%		44%	0%		0%
Dealing w/ Staffing issues	0%		0%	0%		0%	0%		0%
Sales		32%			18%			4%	
Hiring	0%		0%	4%		20%	4%		100%
Training	0%		0%	0%		0%	0%		0%
Keeping	0%		0%	0%		0%	0%		0%
Providing Compensation	0%		0%	0%		0%	0%		0%
Finding effective marketing	29%		89%	14%		80%	0%		0%
Affording marketing	4%		11%	0%		0%	0%		0%
Technical		4%			32%			71%	
Understanding	4%		100%	0%		0%	33%		47%
Finding technology	0%		0%	29%		89%	33%		47%
Affording	0%		0%	4%		11%	4%		6%
Installing/maintain	0%		0%	0%		0%	0%		0%
Financial		46%			18%			4%	
Keeping records	0%		0%	0%		0%	0%		0%
Complying	14%		31%	0%		0%	0%		0%
Obtaining financing	32%		69%	18%		100%	4%		100%

Results for Industry Groups.

CAM-X Members (continued)

CAM-X Members

		Low	High	Ave
1	Year founded:	1945	1988	1971
	Year founded/bought/started:	1956	1989	1976
18	Time in the industry:	5	25	15

		Past		Present		Future	
		%	Count	%	Count	%	Count
2,9,12	Organization viewed as:						
	Telephone Answering Svc	89%	8	22%	2	22%	2
	TeleServices company	11%	1	56%	5	44%	4
	Call Center	0%	0	22%	2	33%	3
			9		9		9

		Number of Accounts	Revenue	Number of Calls	Length of Calls
5,6,7,8	The following items:				
	Increased greatly	63%	56%	56%	22%
	Increased somewhat	0%	22%	22%	44%
	Stayed the same	0%	11%	0%	33%
	Decreased slightly	13%	0%	11%	0%
	Decreased greatly	25%	11%	11%	0%
		100%	100%	100%	100%

		All Answers		Most Likely	
15,16	In the future you plan to:				
	Scale back	7%	1	14%	1
	Position it to be sold	7%	1	0%	0
	Maintain business as is	0%	0	0%	0
	Pursue acquisitions	36%	5	14%	1
	Increase sales & marketing	50%	7	71%	5
			14		7

17	Title/position:		
	Pres, CEO, Owner	67%	6
	Op Mgr, VP Op, Dir Op, GM	33%	3
	Sales Mgr	0%	0
			9

Trend Analysis - Breakdown:		
Past / Present / Future		
TAS / TAS / TAS	11%	1
TAS / TAS / TS	0%	0
TAS / TAS / CC	0%	0
TAS / TS / TAS	0%	0
TAS / TS / TS	44%	4
TAS / TS / CC	11%	1
TAS / CC / CC	22%	2
TS / TAS / TAS	11%	1
TS / TAS / CC	0%	0
CC / CC / CC	0%	0
		9

19	Association memberships (44 responded):		
	ATSI	33%	3
	NAEO	22%	2
	CAM-X	100%	9
	PIN	22%	2
	CEO	0%	0
	SNUG	11%	1
	IVMA	0%	0
	ASTAA	0%	0
	GLTSA	0%	0
	TUNe	0%	0
	WSTA	0%	0

Trend Analysis - Summary:		
Stay the Same	11%	1
Have Changed	67%	6
Will Change	0%	0
Ongoing Change	11%	1
Switch Back to TAS	11%	1
		9

20	Wants To Receive Results:	100%	9

BIBLIOGRAPHY

Allimadi, M. (1999a, May). Telecommuting grows as technology adapts to needs. Call Center Magazine, pp. 90-92.

Allimadi, M. (1999b, May). Web transactions and demand for live agents on the rise. Call Center Magazine, pp. 68-74.

Anderson, J. & Taylor, Z. (1998, September). Uncovering maximum leverage in call center performance. TeleProfessional, pp. 84-88.

Anton, J. (1997). Call center benchmark report. Purdue University, pp. 1-11.

Anton, J. (1999a, September). Research highlights from Purdue University. Call Center Magazine, p. 14.

Anton, J. (1999c). Call center benchmark report. Purdue University, pp. 1-1 – E-4.

Anton, J. & Nickerson, A. (1998, December). Pre-employment agent screening. TeleProfessional, pp. 86-96.

ATSI. (1989). TAS History. Answer, pp. 30-34.

ATSI. (1998, June). ATSI statistical survey, pp. 1-8.

Bianchi, A. (1998, Tech No. 2). Lines of fire. Inc., pp. 36-50.

Blevel, B. (1999, November). TeleProfessional, p. 9.

Charnock, R. (1997, December). CIS in the year 2000. TeleProfessional, p. 34.

Cleveland, B. (1999, April). Dawning of a new era. TeleProfessional, p. 114.

Cleveland, B., & Mayben, J. (1997). Call Center Management on Fast Forward. Annapolis, Maryland: Call Center Press.

DeHaan, P. (1998). The Telephone Answering Service Industry: Preparing for the Future. Los Angeles: KWU

Dresner, S. (1998, March). The web-enabled call center. TeleProfessional, pp. 50-52.

Durr, B. (1999, March). Crafting perfection. TeleProfessional, pp. 32-42.

Elwell, R. (1999, June). When you think "monitoring" think "John Smith." Call Center Solutions, pp. 60-66.

Fentem, L. (1997, December). How to select the right outsourced teleservices partner. TeleProfessional, pp. 46-48.

Fleischer, J. (1998a, November) IP telephony – The newest call center service. Call Center Magazine, pp. 28-30.

Fleischer, J. (1998b, December) Web sites that drive customers to call centers. Call Center Magazine, pp. 97-104.

Fleischer, J. (1999a, February). Essential tools for web-enabling your call center. Call Center Magazine, pp. 81-87.

Fleischer, J. (1999b, June). A host of email services for call centers. Call Center Magazine, pp. 28-32.

Frankl, S. (1999, May). The telechannel hits the mark. TeleProfessional, p. 17.

Frost & Sullivan notes surge in outsourcing. (1999, May). Connections Magazine, p. 34.

Ghio, T. (1999, May). The uncentered call center. Call Center Solutions, pp. 80-88.

Goodman, J. (1998, September). Cross industry group explores pros and cons of call center management certification. TeleProfessional, p. 136.

Gray, G. (1999, January). The future of the teleservices industry? Call Center Solutions, pp. 90-96.

Hickox, G. (1998, March). A marriage made in web heaven. TeleProfessional, pp. 42-48.

Jackson, K. (1998a, July). Leap ahead to excellence. Call Center Magazine, pp. 198-205.

Jackson, K. (1998b, September). Are you misorganized? Call Center Magazine, pp. 113-117.

Kahan, R. (1998, July). Opportunity costs. Telephony, pp.116-134.

Kahn, S. (1999, January). Redefining call center metrics – The quality connection. Call Center Solutions, pp. 106-110.

Karr, A. (1998a, March). The growth of the multimedia call center.

TeleProfessional, pp. 10).

Karr, A. (1998b, December). The prefect fit. TeleProfessional, pp. 59-60).

Karr, A. (1999a, April). Lemons or lemonade? TeleProfessional, pp. 43-47.

Karr, A. (1999b, May). Work at home. TeleProfessional, pp. 68-70.

Karr, A. (1999c, November). Telephone Creates 5M Jobs. TeleProfessional, p. 14.

Klasnic, K. (1997, December). The stars and stripes are flying high: Growth in American call centers. TeleProfessional, pp. 24-26.

Kopf, D. (1999, May). Going virtual. TeleProfessional, pp. 44-52.

Lawrence, L. (1998, March). Call center benchmarking study results. TeleProfessional, pp. 54-58.

Lenz, M. (1999, June). Grappling with agent turnover. Call Center Magazine, p. 6.

Liebeskind, K (1998, June). Get the message. Selling Power, pp. 69-71.

Mandaro, T. & Wilson, S. (1999, May). Call center operations. TeleProfessional, pp. 55-56.

MCI. (1997). Call centers: Success on the line. Strategy and Technology group of NetworkMCI Services [white paper], pp. 1-16.

Mikol, T. (1997, October). Progress toward a customer interaction center. Telemarketing and Call Center Solutions, pp. 70-80.

Mitchell, P. (1998, April) Aligning customer call centers for 2001. Telemarketing and Call Center Solutions, pp. 64-69.

Morrow, M. (1997, October). Cost-justifying call center investments. Telemarketing and Call Center Solutions, pp. 82-88.

Newton, H. (1989). Newton's telecom dictionary: The official glossary of telecommunications acronyms, terms and jargon (2nd ed.). New York: Telecom Library.

Perkins, D. & Anton, J. (1997, April). Best practices for customer service call centers – An exclusive statistical study. Telemarketing and Call Center Solutions, pp. 80-88.

Porter, D. (1999a, April). Call center market trends. TeleProfessional, p. 24.

Porter, D. (1999b, April). Perfecting call center operations. TeleProfessional, pp. 49-51.

Porter, D. (1999c, November). Majority unlikely to trust web sites. TeleProfessional, pp. 12-14.

QueueTips. (1999a, August). [Internet, http://www.ccmreview.com/queuetips_01/qtips_converse.html]

QueueTips. (1999b, August). [Internet, http://www.ccmreview.com/queuetips_01/qtips_tidbits.html]

QueueTips. (1999c, August). [Internet, http://www.ccmreview.com/queuetips_01/qtips_webwatch.html]

QueueTips. (1999d, August). [Internet,

http://www.ccmreview.com/queuetips_02/qtips_webwatch.html]

Read, B. (1998, September). Products to make your small call center look big. Call Center Magazine, pp. 28-42.

Read, B. (1999a, February). Outsourcers to untangle your web needs. Call Center Magazine, pp. 30-38.

Read, B. (1999b, September). Outsourcing your internet service concerns. Call Center Magazine, pp. 98-108.

Reiners, D. (1999, April). Looking forward. TeleProfessional, pp. 33-39.

Reynolds, P. (1999, March). Automating for better workforce management. Call Center Solutions, pp. 74-80.

Riggs, B. & Thyfault, M. (1999, Oct 4). The modern call center. Information Week, pp. 53-68.

Rose, B. (1998, September). The view from here. TeleProfessional, pp. 116-120.

Slater, D. (1999, May 15). Holding patterns. CIO, pp. 54-62.

Sturdy, M. (1997, December). The need for quality assurance will intensify as customer expectations escalate. TeleProfessional, p. 33.

Sweat, J. (1999, October 4). Human touch. Information Week, pp. 18-19.

Tamar, M. (1996, July/August). Quality as a competitive differentiator. TeleProfessional, pp. 24-26.

Tehrani, N. (1997, November). Outsourcing...A prudent way to do business. Telemarketing and Call Center Solutions, pp. 2-4.

Tehrani, N. (1998, September). Will internet marketing replace direct marketing? Telemarketing and Call Center Solutions, pp. 2-6.

Theis, P. (1999a, May 3). Transforming your call center into a profit center. Teleservices News, p. 17.

Theis, P. (1999b, June). Is your service agency feeding you a line? TeleProfessional, pp. 59-60.

Thornton, S. (1999a, June). Teleservices in 2000. TeleProfessional, p. 9.

Thornton, S. (1999b, June). Call center operations. TeleProfessional, pp. 64-68.

Toledo, L. (1999, May 3). Selecting technology to create a leading-edge call center. Teleservices News, p. 17.

Volpe, L. (1999, May). Distributed call centers move into the decade of intimacy. Call Center Solutions, pp. 92-97.

Wortman, V. (1999, November). Call center building blocks. TeleProfessional, pp. 16-20.

Wood, J. (1997, December). The future of customer service: The web subsumes the telephone. TeleProfessional, p. 33.

Young, D. (1998, March). The facts about outsourcing and financial performance. TeleProfessional, pp. 62-64.